Poetic Voices Without Borders

Edited by Robert L. Giron

Arlington, Virginia

Copyright © 2005 by Gival Press, LLC.

Introduction © 2005 by Robert L. Giron.

All rights reserved under International and Pan-American Copyright Conventions. Printed in the United States of America.

With the exception of brief quotations in the body of critical articles or reviews, no part of this book may be reproduced or transmitted in any form or by any means, graphic, electronic, or mechanical, including photocopying, recording, taping, or by any information storage or retrieval system, without the permission in writing from the publisher.

After publication, all rights revert to the individual poets.

Published by Gival Press, an imprint of Gival Press, LLC.

For information please write:
Gival Press, LLC, P. O. Box 3812, Arlington, VA 22203.

Website: *www.givalpress.com*
Email: givalpress@yahoo.com

First edition ISBN 1-928589-30-8
Library of Congress Control Number: 2005924500

Bookcover artwork *Conversational Peace* Copyright © 2004 by Joel Traylor.
Format and design by Ken Schellenberg.

en memoria de mi querida tía Ventura Valdez y Campolla Marmolejo

Contents

Introduction -------------------------- by Robert L. Giron - - 11
when it drops you gonna feel it ---------- by Karren L. Alenier - - 14
spiritual what if ---------------------- by Assef Al-Jundi - - 14
lavender wedding --------------------- by Shane Allison - - 15
nomad of silence ----------------- by Luis Alberto Ambroggio - - 16
undesirable things --------------- by Luis Alberto Ambroggio - - 16
ambivalence ------------------------- by John Amen - - 17
"poetry sucks!" -------------------------- by Antler - - 17
transplant --------------------- by Rosanna Armendariz - - 18
airing my house ----------------------- by Scott Bailey - - 19
things a depressed person cannot do ------------ by Sally Ball - - 20
in which we serve --------------------- by Greg Baysans - - 20
instructions after death --------------- by Gabriella Belfiglio - - 21
hunger -------------------------------- by Mel Belin - - 23
the outing to the temple of body parts --------- by Linda Bieler - - 23
blind eyes --------------------- by Morrigan Benton-Floyd - - 24
postcards in pencil ---------------------- by Larry Blazek - - 25
to my children ------------------- by Jeanell Buida Bolton - - 25
speak to water ------------------------- by Jody Bolz - - 26
clear thoughts in the middle of my 33rd year by Louis E. Bourgeois - - 27
blankets -------------------------- by Janet I. Buck - - 27
companionate marriage --------------- by Cathleen Calbert - - 28
cartoon coyote goes po-mo --------------- by Brenda Cárdenas - - 29
the history beneath our skin ------------ by Brenda Cárdenas - - 30
poem for the tin-tun-teros -------------- by Brenda Cárdenas - - 31
zacuanpapalotls --------------------- by Brenda Cárdenas - - 31
my sweet onion --------------------- by Carol Carpenter - - 32
this is everything i did not want to feel ------- by Grace Cavalieri - - 33
frida paints her portrait looking in a mirror ------ by Don Cellini - - 34
what borges told me ------------------- by Don Cellini - - 35
starkweather: june 25, 1959 ----------- by Christopher Conlon - - 35
in the absence of knowing ------------------ by Nina Corwin - - 36
the fluorescent range funeral home ------------ by Jim Curran - - 37
the boar tracks fading --------------------- by G. L. Curtis - - 38
proper geometry ---------------------- by Jill Darling - - 38
false starts for cursed letters --------- by Mitchell L. H. Douglas - - 39
mister on the angels --------------------- by Jim Elledge - - 40
napoleon ------------------------- by J. Glenn Evans - - 41
on the road to el paso ----------------- by Manuel Figuroa - - 42
there / here --------------------------- by Steven Finch - - 43
undocumented --------------- by Maureen Tolman Flannery - - 44
my father typing --------------------- by Gretchen Fletcher - - 45
don't mourn. organize! --------------- by H. Susan Freireich - - 45

ivana, the queen of prague	by Mary L. Gardner --46
gift	by Bernadette Geyer --47
where the *air is beyond happiness*	by John Gilgun --47
the letting go	by Robert L. Giron --48
that bitch-goddess	by Paula Goldman --49
lyrics	by Jewelle Gomez --50
running home from school	by Jewelle Gomez --51
poem for the brother you never had	by John Grey --52
holding hands	by Benjamin Scott Grossberg --53
eyes of wax	by JoseMarGuerr --54
letter of denunciation	by Piotr Gwiazda --55
the choice	by Piotr Gwiazda --55
on a bench: my life	by Myronn Hardy --56
the last world of fire and trash	by Joy Harjo --57
navigating the warning	by Joy Harjo --58
reality show	by Joy Harjo --59
after-dinner remarks	by suzan shown harjo --60
aria	by Daniel Hefko --61
anima	by Wendy Hilsen-Bernard --62
june 15 (from *As Experience*)	by Laura Hinton --63
terror travels	by Walter Holland --63
louisiana	by Peter Huggins --63
route 501 south	by Lucas Jacob --64
acapulco	by John Jenkison --65
death food	by Fran Jordan --66
temazcal	by Claire Joysmith --67
my jar of leeches	by Jacqueline Jules --68
this time of sand and teeth (Make Peace Not War)	by Gunilla Theander Kester --68
pennies in a cracked cup	by Peter Klappert --69
fall evening	by George Klawitter --71
honor among soldiers	by Randy Koch --72
impressionists	by Teresa Joy Kramer --73
secrets	by Bruce Lader --74
watching your sleeping face	by Mary Ann Larkin --75
the rain	by Daniel W. K. Lee --75
reporting from fallujah	by Gary Lehmann --76
over café	by Raina J. León --76
moonrise, hernandez, new mexico 1941	by Lyn Lifshin --77
i am a shoe	by Raymond Luczak --78
throwaway kid	by Steven Manchester --78
oasis	by Jeff Mann --79
1962	by Jaime Manrique - 80
return to the country of my birth	by Jaime Manrique --81
in the garden of lope de vega	by C. M. Mayo --82
passage	by Judith McCombs --83
platinum-blond dharma	by Michael Meyerhofer --83
the games children play	by E. Ethelbert Miller --84

silent reading — by Larry Moffi — 85
birds of paradise — by Ron Mohring — 86
to erica: transgendered — by Albert J. Montesi — 87
on *día de los muertos* neruda speaks to me — by Kay Murphy — 87
el campo — by Victoria Bosch Murray — 88
dusk on the ridge — by Yvette Neisser — 89
erosion — by Daniel Pantano — 89
military fantasia — by Richard Peabody — 90
water round the ring of fire of indonesia — by James Penha — 91
mosquito blizzard — by Kenneth Pobo — 92
side effects — by Adrian S. Potter — 92
la loca de la playa puerto
    escondido, mexico — by Emmanuelle Pourroy-Braud — 93
premonitions — by Maria Proitsaki — 94
lightning in wartime — by Tony Reevy — 95
the back of my hand — by Kim Roberts — 96
modern malaise — by Peter Roberts — 97
whitmanesque — by J. E. Robinson — 97
buddha breathes — by Joseph Ross — 98
numbers — by Marianne Ehrlich Ross — 98
he was a poet and when he died — by Mark Saba — 99
puzzles — by Jhoanna Salazar — 99
che bel rimedio — by V. Jane Scheeloch — 100
moskva — by Keith Scotcher — 101
january — by Gregg Shapiro — 102
naming — by Marian Kaplun Shapiro — 103
you don't believe that dromedaries
    keep moonlight in their humps? — by Lucille Gang Shulklapper — 104
harmless — by Myra Sklarew — 105
for contemporary historians — by J.D. Smith — 105
on ice — by Reet Sool — 106
help — by Laurel Speer — 107
voyage — by Judith Strasser — 107
saxophone — by Dan Stryk — 108
november and november and november — by John Sweet — 109
why i love florence — by Hilary Tham — 110
what moves us — by Hilary Tham — 110
bicoastal: the sell date on my life has expired — by Gloria Vando — 111
positive images — by Shelley Ann Wake — 112
finally in autumn — by Davi Walders — 113
reunion — by Amelia Walker — 113
lying in bed — by Jeff Walt — 114
miss kitty's blues — by Jeff Walt — 115
to my ex-lover making a commitment — by Jeff Walt — 115
coming home — by Charlotte Warren — 116
passing as a mulatto — by Allison Whittenberg — 117
dora circa the war years — by Allison Whittenberg — 117
nights before christmas — by Fred A. Wilcox — 118

asking directions ----------------------- by Jill Williams - 119
pure jazz --------------------------- by A. D. Winans - 119
an arab dreamer and i dream the same dream by Ernie Wormwood - 120
loki ------------------------------- by Gerard Wozek - 120
the country of us ---------------------- by H. E. Wright - 121
language of the earth ---------------- by Katharina Yakovina - 122

French Poems

la musique ----------------------- par Robert L. Giron - 125
dans un sac en osier ------------------ par Colette Michael - 125
l'autre face de l'empire -------- par Mutombo Nkulu-N'Sengha - 126
l'astronome ---------------- par Emmanuelle Pourroy-Braud - 127
errant -------------------- par Emmanuelle Pourroy-Braud - 128
panégyrique pour l'emmerdeur ------------- par G. Tod Slone - 128
sous appellation contrôlée... dite liberté ------- par G. Tod Slone - 129
enfin en automne ---------------------- par Davi Walders - 130

Spanish Poems

al poeta que sobreviva ------------ por Luis Alberto Ambroggio - 133
inocencia ------------------------- por José Ben-Kotel - 133
la casa del anón --------------------- por Leonel P. Bernal - 135
ansias --------------------------- por Leonel P. Bernal - 136
después de tanto ----------------------- por Rei Berroa - 136
la verdad a todas horas --------------------- por Rei Berroa - 137
al mestizaje ---------------------- por Brenda Cárdenas - 138
poema para los tin-tun-teros ------------ por Brenda Cárdenas - 138
desde el beso del tiempo ---------- por Fanny Carrión de Fierro - 139
esta voz --------------------- por Fanny Carrión de Fierro - 140
frida pinta su retrato mirándose en un espejo ---- por Don Cellini - 141
lo que me dijo borges --------------------- por Don Cellini - 142
san andrés de la cal ---------------------- por Don Cellini - 143
la luz azul ---------------------------- por Alfred Corn - 143
respuesta a darío ----------------------- por Alfred Corn - 144
lenguaje sin fronteras ------------------- por Efraín Garza - 144
triste panorama --------------------- por Efraín Garza - 145
lejos de todos ---------------------- por Robert L. Girón - 145
a ritmo de discoteca ------------------ por Juan M. Godoy - 146
la carrera del guardacostas -------------- por Juan M. Godoy - 147
vi a las estrellas echándome
    la culpa con la noche ------------ por Rigoberto González - 147
ojos de cera ------------------------- por JoseMarGuerr - 148
laberintos --------------------- por Marta López-Luaces - 149
llegar ----------------------- por Marta López-Luaces - 149
manhattan ----------------------- por Jaime Manrique - 150
chantal -------------------- por Benito Pastoriza Iyodo - 152
borecua blues ----------------- por Maritza Rivera Cohen - 152

no al silencio ----------------------- por Irving Rodríguez - 153
evolución ----------------------- por Rose Mary Salum - 154
buenos aires, 2002 ----------------- por Silvia R. Tandeciarz - 154
ecuador ----------------------- por Silvia R. Tandeciarz - 156
galápagos --------------------- por Silvia R. Tandeciarz - 157
velázquez pinta en color por primera vez ----- por Sheila Tombe - 158
borinquen --------------------------- por Gloria Vando - 159

The Poets -- 161

Introduction

How often have you picked up a journal or anthology of poetry hoping to find something new and instead find that the voices or styles in the volume are pretty much the same? I'm not trying to suggest that journals or magazines should not have a set style they are trying to promote; however, when I began thinking about putting an anthology of poetry together over a year ago, I wanted to do something different. I wanted to create an anthology that would not necessarily fall into some predetermined category or style. Instead, I envisioned a collection of poetry that would literally transcend *borders,* on a variety of metamorphical senses, which would use *poetic voices* to do it.

First, being trilingual (English/Spanish/French), I knew that I wanted the anthology to represent the three major languages of North America but which also happened to be part of my cultural heritage, even if on my father's side of the family I am a fifth generation American. To include original poetry written in these three languages by Americans or others speaks to my second reason for the anthology; that is, to encourage the reading and writing in these languages. Though I grew up hearing English and Spanish spoken in family situations, it is sad to say that I am one of few in my family who have continued to maintain Spanish fluency. Knowing at a very young age that languages fascinated me, I eventually picked up French in high school and college and have re-cultivated it since I discovered very distant French Giron cousins in Lorraine, France in 1996. Finally, the third reason for this anthology was to give poets an opportunity to voice what they have to say, be it personal, social, or political.

I knew I wanted to reach beyond the ordinary. When I first heard Grace Cavalieri's poem *This Is Everything I Did Not Want to Feel (in the voice of Mary Wollstonecraft 1759-1797),* it intrigued me because here is a fine example of a poet who is speaking in a voice from the past and who is transcending the *border* of time.

> I wanted a crescendo of women
> Saying: *There is enough for all ...*
> We will walk through the dark of this house.
> Words will seep through the walls. We are able.
> There is a light on the hill we can walk through.
>
> Women everywhere are aching.
>
> I would preach a ballad from the roof,
> Sing to the mermaids and children,
> Cross limbs with scholars,

Leave footprints in the snow,
Write the weeds of our history,
Bring our pieces together. That is what I wanted.

Whereas it is not uncommon for poets to take on the persona of another person, it perhaps is a bit less common for poets to speak for someone who is dead and who is not close to our own time period. This reminds me of a poem I wrote about my maternal grandmother's encounter with the bandit Pancho Villa near the Río Grande years after she told me her story. However, what Cavalieri has accomplished not only in this poem but also in her collection from which it is a part is to give the deceased a voice in the present so that we might be able to better understand the person and time in which she lived.

In keeping with this transcending of borders, Assef Al-Jundi's poem *Spiritual What If* asks about the brutal effect of religion upon people or perhaps the abuse by people of the spiritual because it is impossible to separate religion from culture and politics, or simply money and power. In Greg Bayans' poem *In Which We Serve* we are confronted with the complexities of religion and sex.

In this anthology there are numerous examples of poets who report the present with all its complexities in terms of gender (see Shane Allison's *Lavender Wedding*), place (see Rosana Armendariz's *Transplant* or Jaime Manrique's *Return to the Country of My Birth*), war (see Mel Belin's *Hunger* or Steven Finch's *There / Here*), aging (see Jeanell Buida Bolton's *To My Children*), relationships (see Cathleen Calbert's *Companionate Marriage* or Jeff Walt's poems), cultural and social struggle (see Brenda Cárdenas' poems or Jewelle Gomez's *Running Home from School* or the work by Joy Harjo or Suzan Shown Harjo), death (see Gary Lehmann's *Reporting from Fallujah* or Marianne Ehrlich Ross's *Numbers*), personal identity (see Allison Whittenberg's *Passing as a Mulatto*), music (see A. D. Winans' *Pure Jazz* or Dan Stryk's *Saxophone*), art (see the work by Paula Goldman or Don Cellini), in short, life in general, but with an edge.

What the poets in this anthology have in common is that they are willing to take a risk to say what needs to be said, and I hope this anthology has given them the platform in which to say it well, without someone placing them into a category or market because they are male, female, straight, gay, white, black, Native American, liberal, conservative, religious, non-religious, pro-war, anti-war, young, middle-aged, old, American, Latin American, European, Asian, African, Australian, rich, poor, widely published or an emerging poet.

Back in 1979 when I studied comparative literature and criticism, I vowed to stress as a poet and a future publisher that it is essential for readers to recognize the value of a *work*, which should be the center of any literary criticism, and to let the *work* speak for itself.

Et voilà, I invite you to read these poems which I'm sure will captivate you.

—RLG

when it drops you gonna feel it
by Karren L. Alenier

We traded
Internet for mosquito
net, cocooned
for sleep
under a halo
of white mesh
the sea beating
the coral cliffs
of Negril—a lullaby
of dominoes, geckos,
the kingpins in the road
hawking anything-you-want,
the minstrel Fire improvising
Toots Hibbert's *Pressure Drop*,
a daughter hopeful that her father
in a Sav-la-Mar hospital would kick
lung cancer with an herbal medicine
something six chemo treatments
in Georgia couldn't do.

spiritual what if
by Assef Al-Jundi

If we had not had
Jesus, Muhammad,
Moses and all the other
do-gooders,
we may have been
better off.
We wouldn't need to ponder
which day is a Sabbath,
whether to turn
the other cheek
or take the other fellow's
eye out,
how many times a day to pray,
or what kinds of orgies
await us in heaven.

I don't know if sacrificing virgins,
worshipping the sun,

or exalting gods
made of colored beads
is better?
Halliburton may still have
the inside track in Iraq?
Jihadies of the Vengeance Deity
could still be doing battle
with warriors of the Holy Dollar?

Perhaps
poets,
sinners,
and non-believers
always had it right?

lavender wedding
by Shane Allison

I'm convinced that I'll get married in the gym of my old high school.
The ceremony will take place on a beautiful spring afternoon
on Saturday 'cause Saturdays are for weddings.
My suit will be *virgin* white with a shirt of lavender and ruffles at the collar.
The shoes will be plat-formed.
I'll reek of Brut and Afro-sheen.
My husband to be will look stunning
in his lavender Christian Dior wedding dress imported from Paris.
I'll mow the hair from my legs like newly cut grass with a Lady Bic.
Pluck my chest hairs like feathers from a chicken.
Paint these lips with apple red lipstick.
I want all my closest friends to come ornamented in those dresses
like they wore in *Footloose*.
My lesbian friends will come dressed as Wall Street tycoons
constantly reminding me how expensive all this shit is
and how much it's going to set me back
no matter how many times I tell them that money is no object.
I want my Daddy to give me away
if he promises to keep his hands off Aunt Tillie.
My Mama will be the barer of rice and punch spiked with whiskey.
The priest will be a Michael Jackson impersonator.
The reception will be held at the House of Chicken and Waffles.
where Debbie, employee of the month, will catch the bouquet.
Wally, the four hundred pound, stubble- faced cook,
who smokes stink cigars, where the ashes
occasionally fall in the blueberry pancake mix,
will have the pleasure of pulling the garter belt
from my husband's thigh with his teeth.

There will be no limousines 'cause if a Pinto was good
enough for my sister and her husband,
it's good enough for me and mine.

nomad of silence
by Luis Alberto Ambroggio
      translation by C. M. Mayo

Soon the bridges will disappear
rivers, seas will swallow the earth
we will go begging, if at all
air for eyes
wind over the muteness of the sands.

And what can I do with the waters
with these islands of dark rock
with the famished clouds that float past
gray with sadness.

Before marching to the dunes
nomad in silence
if Keats could hear me
if even wise Jefferson were listening
I would shout
with the choked voice of the desert
"I prefer to write aimlessly
than to write in desperation."

undesirable things
by Luis Alberto Ambroggio
      translation by Yvette Neisser

This light of ice.
The mildew that invades the naked thigh.
The voices that disappear
        in the ambush of days.
The rite of lighting candles for rain,
        for noise or for any other promise.
The rust of invoked shadows.
Unpardonable sins.
The mute wake of fire.
Fingernails with fresh blood.
Defeat.

ambivalence
by John Amen

Darkness and dawn wrestled in the alley.
The yucca bloomed as bridges collapsed.

The singer had forgotten his lyrics,
and rain was flooding from an electric sky.

I have destroyed enough for one lifetime.

Summer faded like a tattoo.
Reluctance exploded like ballet.

Everywhere I looked I saw torn bibles,
hymnals scattered in a gutter. The sun
sank into the ocean like a burning anchor.

When I came to, I was holding a shotgun.

"poetry sucks!"
by Antler

The word "sucks" is being abused
    by being used
        derogatorily,
The word "sucks" molested by youths
    under the age of consent
        insulting
Poetry and babies and cocksuckers alike
    not to mention adult titsuckers,
        tongue-suckers, thumb-suckers, toe-suckers,
    nose and earlobe-suckers, sucker suckers
        and trees who suck the earth
    and butterflies who suck flowers
        and black holes who suck galaxies.
Like it or not, boys in every state of America
    in every city every town
        when poetry is mentioned
    say "Poetry sucks!"
Cute youths who never got sucked
    and have no inkling of blowjobjoy
        taking advantage of
    the word "sucks"
        putting poetry down—

True, poetry sucks, but not derogatorily.
Poetry sucks beautifully, beautiful
    as a blowjob tongue swirling
        round the most sensitive spots.
And guess what?
Every day poets all over Earth
    compose thousands of brand-new
        100% guaranteed cocksucking hymns
    that swell the accumulated
        immortal poetry of the ages.
Yeah, Poetry sucks: Poetry exposes itself
    to punks who sneer "Poetry sucks!"
        in the image of a big blowjob
    that gives them instantaneous hardons
        that won't be satisfied
    till they get their first suck.
No problem.
Enough poets exist—men, boys, women, girls—
    to help out.
Give a blowjob to every boy who says
    "Poetry sucks!"
Simple as that!

transplant
by Rosanna Armendariz

To live in the Borderlands means you
drink tequila and mescal
in bars and at weddings,
or alone at night to soothe the little devils poking at the souls of your feet,
until one day, you don't want that slow dance with death anymore.

To live in the Borderlands means you
tried cocaine for the first time at age twenty four,
given to you by a spirit,
Lobo,
a partial albino with mismatched eyes,
who made love to you hard and fast
on the bathroom floor,
in his car,
on your ex-husband's bed,
until morning rose like a black angel
and you prayed for sleep.

To live in the Borderlands means you
like the taste of dirt in your mouth and

the feel of wind on your face,
setting off car alarms and
knocking down signs.

To live in the Borderlands means you
drink and you snort and you spit,
reaching for that warm someone,
licking the salt from her thighs.

To live in the Borderlands means you
hate skyscrapers and crowded subway cars,
that you want desert,
sprawl, sand, cacti,
anonymity,
that's why you stay.

airing my house
by Scott Bailey

Desire is fruit in crisis—
the flesh peeled by preachers—

but my butter still churns for a friend
(I can't print his name)

whose bait catches in my mouth,
after his four-wheeler

zips us over a bridge
and over a hill of briars

shadowing a creek
where we skinny dip,

where hands,
schooling between each others' legs,

reduce sermons to cold irons
failing to straighten our creases out.

things a depressed person cannot do
by Sally Ball

Wait in line at the Division of Motor Vehicles.
Purchase mayonnaise.
Speak a foreign language.

Tolerate an infant;
a spouse's weakness;
more than one noise at a time (voice + dishwasher, say,
or t.v. + magazine page);
any noise in a room with a tile floor;
synthetic fabric, especially on the skin of the arms.

Nor: Flirt

Protect

Console

Seduce

in which we serve
by Greg Baysans

J-'s leather jacket and blue jeans fit
as well on Wednesday as did the collar
he wore to work on Sundays.

It was a Wednesday, and in the bar
the boy was speaking the Spanish of
J-'s extra Mass each Saturday.

They spoke. They left together.
They didn't speak of what each did
in service to God or Mammon.

Climaxing in the safety of darkness,
the boy muttered a low, unintended,
"Gracias, Diosito*, gracias."

---

* Diosito: diminutive form of God

instructions after death
by Gabriella Belfiglio

1. Save one part of the firewood of my body—
   You choose:
   hand, nipple, elbow, spleen, heart, clitoris.

2. Offer the remainder to science—
   what's still functioning, give away,
   answer someone's prayer.
   If it is too late, bring my body
   to a hospital with eager students,
   let me touched one more time,
   eyes curious to see what's inside.

   Let them cut open, past skin,
   and like a poem in a foreign language,
   read each recognizable vein, follow
   the skinny slippery route up my thick thigh
   down my solid spine,
   make a sliver of sense of our mysterious body.

(My only restriction is that no piece of me go
to cosmetic plastic surgery.)

3. Burn the part you saved.
   Have song in the background,
   like at a campfire—Joni Mitchell or Nina Simone.
   If my brother is alive, rent a grand piano
   for him to play.

4. Separate the ashes into three.

5. Carry a third to Italy, here you must
   measure out a teaspoon of the dried basil of my body
   sprinkle it into the Arno river,
   under that massive weeping willow
   there on the edge of Florence.

   With the remainder, head south.
   Keep me in your pocket.
   Walk around the streets,
   look up and down instead of left and right.
   Notice the art under your feet,
   the colors above your head.

   Talk to people on the way,

use your eyes, your hands, the tilt of your head,
don't use English.
As you walk away, say:
sta mi bene, your fingers still reaching.

After you find Mt. Etna growing
out of the tiny village of Randazzo, shed the rest of me.
There will be ash here already, mix mine in
with bare hands—like when you make meatballs.
Give it a little spit in place of egg to make it stick.

6. Return to America.

7. Retrieve the second third.

    If it is winter, head to the Brooklyn Bridge.
    Here you must have a plan.

    It is not as easy as you might think to fling
    contents into the East River.
    There are cars zooming below you,
    a web of metal enclosing you—throw strong
    with a full arc of motion.

    If it is summer, take the F train to Coney Island.
    Buy something awful, like cotton candy
    or a Nathan's hot dog, or battered
    fried shrimp with more batter than shrimp.
    Maybe go on a ride or two. (I would do this
    first, however).
    Sit in the sun, and when you are ready
    run past the mass of people, past the shallow waves,
    till you can dive into the Atlantic Ocean whole—
    empty me here.

8. With the third part of my ashes,
   go to Philadelphia, where I started.
   Find Giovanni's Room, sit by the window,
   read someone remarkable
   like Audre Lorde or Adrienne Rich.
   If you find my book, read
   something from here too.
   Afterwards, find a private area of Fairmont Park.
   And with a seed of your favorite tree,
   bury me.

hunger
by Mel Belin

On a mountain hillside, two battalions move
into the open,
training tanks and howitzers on rebels
that cross the border . . . It's all presented
matter-of-factly in the front page
of a paper I read on a park-bench
in early June . . .
                  shelling, slaughtering
to stop their incursion,
even as a third force of B-52s overhead
begin to drop 500 pound Mark-82 gravity
and cluster bombs pulverizing
the attackers, who nonsensically continue
to press forward to engage . . .
Beside me, a wasp buzzes—
maybe it's after my cranberry muffin,
or the aroma of the coffee . . .
                        I can brush it off,
but not that image, like a dance,
an horrific *pas de trois*
out of J. Henri Fabre: how such a wasp,
Philanthus, with a honey bee mortally
trapped in its mouth,
is seized by a preying mantis
who, with naked triangular head,
begins devouring
the attacker's belly.
                      Even in the final throes
of extinction, a terrible
hunger: *Philanthus* squeezes
the crop of the bee,
which then extends full-length its tongue,
disgorges onto it such delicious
syrup. The wasp licks there to the last.

the outing to the temple of body parts
by Linda Bieler

Orchards and villages dot the hillside.
One street to the top winds past tarps, their spices
drying in the sun.
There are no guards at this temple,

no one here to rent sashes.
The dominion here precedes that.

Children run, following me. I don't know what
to step on:
the phallic assurances,
cunts open right on the sidewalk
ready to catch a heavenly rain of sperm.

The alice in wonderland anatomy book in rock
too odd to touch.
I skirt the shapes and walk along the leaves.

I'm here with no guide
the walkway, a perfunctory clearing
where translucent notes chime
from temple bells
at a single souvenir stand,
the floating parcels in puffs of afternoon light.

We draw but we do
not choose the paint.
Beyond the hills,

the jealous blue dives into red
making a purple compromise, then
a promise of blue and red.

blind eyes
by Morrigan Benton-Floyd

Many would accuse you
Of being a typical macho Mexican
They would see with blind eyes
What machismo really is

There is a power in your pride
Of your family
Of your culture
Of your place in the Universe

Many would accuse you
Of being too arrogant
Controlling your world
They question your ability to love me

There is a power in your love
That protects me
That nurtures me
That finds my power

Many eyes miss
The magic of male energy
That flows through you
Surrounding me with grace

postcards in pencil
by Larry Blazek

I write my friends postcards in pencil
if i use an eraser before
the mail runs the next day
I can take back anger and hasty words
and rub the hurt away.

to my children
by Jeanell Buida Bolton

When I am old, so very old I stink
Of unwashed underarms and brain cell death,
So old I shake, my spine and stature shrink,
I whistle, quake and rattle with each breath—
When I am old, so very old I drool,
And age spots big as elephants appear,
When I forget my name and act the fool
And talk too loud because I cannot hear—
Even when I'm angry, trapped in rage,
Become a miser, call each dime misspent,
When I am cruel and stupid with my age,
When I reject you, scotch your good intent—
      Remember once I loved you of my will,
        And in my heart of hearts, I love you still.

speak to water
by Jody Bolz

In the seconds before his pebble
thwaps well water
how many feet below
startling the air all around him
startling him
the child looks down in
says *hello*
                    lolololo

I would speak to water
if I believed
water listens
instead of half-believing

if I thought my own reflection
no mere play of light
but a rejoinder
transparent and dazzling

if it were true
to my intentions
truer than the voices
I love but misconstrue
direct as an echo
and more transforming

something to make me look again
at my own question
the posture it suggests
something to make
every beauty possible
if not by magic
then by clarity and motion.

I would speak
if I could learn from water
anything like patience:
the steady force of it.

clear thoughts
in the middle of my 33rd year
by Louis E. Bourgeois

One day you'll wake up
in this blue room,
and all will be as shadows,
shadows upon a wall.
Outside the window,
the flowers will turn purple,
and the dog barking
at the edge of town
will lie down and be silent.
The chairs, the books, the tables,
the lamps and clocks
will consume you,
as they mutter their
one coherent message
in your mother tongue:
le monde n'éxiste pas,
nous ne sommes jamais nés.

blankets
by Janet I. Buck

> "The best friendships are the kind where your arms
> can't distinguish burden from embrace."—Laura Italiano

Long ago, we pierced our ears
with a sewing needle and a tough potato
copped from the fridge.
We wiped off the blood in the holes,
passed it around from girl to girl,
applied some alcohol and ice.
Pain was then an erasable fact
made better as each dawn arrived.

Old age is the fortune of a one-way street.
Our midnight chats are fueled
by feuds with body parts.
Nothing to grab that stays but agape's ear
pressed softly to the slowing lung.
A ringing phone — then some siren
going off to mute the lullaby's breath.
Stories in the drying moss.

Our laughter is now listless and lean.
We're caught in a poignant place
of slipping health, fading
like portraits left in the sun.
Moons grow thin as doily cloths
and prayer is where we go
to hold the dropping hand.

companionate marriage
by Cathleen Calbert

Can love conquer time or TV?
Mutability? Matrimony?

Should we divorce
and live in sin? Of course,

I shouldn't even have sex
with a man. We ought to leave

the sword between us that divides
my seventy-nine cents from your dollar,

my glass ceiling from your CEO,
all the U.S. presidents from my big fat zero.

Except I wanted ceremony. (You too.)
Thus: the old-fashioned bloodwork

to shelter children we won't have
and the ridiculous visual check

to see if we're stricken with VD
or packing the proper equipment

(you go out, I go in),
then figs in cream and flute-playing,

hitched by my Scientology minister of a sister,
vows carried away on your parents' breeze.

Beginning with rites like these,
our union is doomed, don't you think?

Seriously, can one ever hope
for better than serial monogamy?

In any case, we're able to conjure
lust occasionally as affectionate equals

although you rarely do the dishes
(or dust or vacuum), and, I confess,

you're the one I'm rudest to.
Does this sum up something?

What can I say in the twenty-first century?
How dare I try to find the words?

Yet you are my Rockefeller grant,
NEA, Guggenheim, Whiting.

Ah, love, let us be
happy together, so happy together.

Let me not admit . . . Let me count . . .
Love me two times, baby.

Love me tender.
I am your wife and friend.

cartoon coyote goes po-mo
by Brenda Cárdenas

Coyote, he never learned the high concept.
He's still rapping at rave parties,
skate-boarding under deconstruction,
past computer networks
(keeps his Olivetti electric in the closet).
Everyone wonders when he'll catch up
like his sister, the computer hacking CEO
of a major pharmaceutical company.
Baby, hers are smart drugs—
performance art provocateurs
tricking the tricksters,
not the white heat Coyote shoots, snorts, swallows.
Hey honey, I can fly
through Ginsberg's naked streets at dawn.
Coyote, he don't quite get it,
applies queer theory to his reading
of Burroughs riding freight train.
In a post-structuralist world
you ride on top of the axles,

underneath either end of a boxcar
and watch the sparks fly!
Don't get a cinder in your eye.
That's the cyberpunk way to get
your mojado butt from the frontera
to the fields or the service sweatshops.
Only if coyote don't find you first,
and if he does, he'll eat you alive,
crunch you down like chicharrón
because he don't want no
vegan dietary restrictions;
no one gonna lay that trip on him.
He'd rather gorge himself on your sweet meat
until he auto-deconstructs,
blows himself to bits
all up and down the Rio Grande.
And in the time it takes you to find
his plastic voodoo in your Lucky Charms,
he'll be warming a stool in the cantina
at the next border town.
How's that for signification theory?

the history beneath our skin
by Brenda Cárdenas

I press the heels of my palms, lean all my weight
into your muscle coiled from neck to waist.

A spring that wound around its prey and snuck
beneath taut skin to breed, this clutching snake.

What memory does it pinch, which lies tangle?
What grief is struck in the rainstorm of its tail?

Is it the cannery heat—thick, sour and damp;
Is it your father's fingers, bent and cramped?

Is it the dust that skims the vines of grapes,
constricting lungs and cutting breath's escape?

Is it the hiss that skirts the river turf,
forks its wire tongue to pierce and split the earth?

Is it your scars, the tracks ancestors scratched,
crossing both countries lashed tight to your back?

Which layers might you shed, which seeds of shame?
Which nightmares nest between your shoulder blades?

If I unsnarl the branches, grasp your pain,
will you tell me your stories, speak their names?

And if my kiss of hands opens your heart,
what poisoned hatchling will slide from my throat?

poem for the tin-tun-teros
by Brenda Cárdenas

This for the timbaleros, percussionists, tin-tun-teros,
those who tap with spoons on their stoves
with pencils on their desks
with nails and knuckles on tables, beds, their own heads
with fists against walls
and fingers on the spines and curves of their lovers, dancers.

This for the congueros, drummers, bongoseros,
those who never rest
with their staccato heels always hammering the skin of the floor
stomping in their dreams filled with maracas, güiros and claves,
these dancers with steps so smooth
and hips that move like their high hats and snares.

This for the timbaleros, percussionists, tin-tun-teros.
They are bad asses with their cymbal storms
their games of sticks that fly like wings. How scampish
their tricks that won't let us work or sleep
only dance and sing, sing and dance
and sometimes move the earth a little.

zacuanpapalotls
(in memory of José Antonio Burciaga, 1947-1996)
by Brenda Cárdenas
    "We are chameleon. We become chameleon."
        —José Antonio Burciaga

We are space between—
the black-orange blur
of a million Monarchs

on their three-generation migration
South to fir-crowned Michoacán
where tree trunks will sprout feathers,
a forest of paper thin wings.

Our dead Mexica cocooned
in the membranes de la Madre Tierra
say we are reborn zacuanpapalotls,
mariposas negras y anaranjadas,
whose whisper of flight
deepens the drum of our lives.

We are between—
the flicker of a chameleon's tail
that turns his desert blue backbone
to jade or pink sand,
the snake skinned fraternal twins
of solstice and equinox.

The silvering dusk, ashen dawn,
la oracíon as it leaves the lips,
first moment of sleep,
the glide into dreams
that husk our mestizo memory.

We are—
one life passing through the prism
of all others, gathering color
to leave an iridescent word,
a rhythm scattered on the wind
like mariposa wings, their dust
tinting the tips of fingers
as they slip into their new light.

my sweet onion
by Carol Carpenter

Ah, sweet Vidalia,
my wild onion child,
I watch your bare feet
root in this Georgia field
as your golden-brown legs
draw nourishment from red clay
days under sun, a harsh spotlight

as you twirl from row
to row full of bulbs and seeds
bursting through soil, cultivated
by you whose grasshopper legs
leap lettuce leaves nibbled
by deer who eat from your hand
when you whisper in their ears

your plans, the rhythm of your heart
pumping visions of pirouettes
on stage where you strengthen
toes, muscles tough enough
as you whirl along the side
of your rented shack, performing
for family who hum, play the harmonica

while you, sweet Vidalia, ride
each note until it holds you,
a season of layers circled under
your translucent skin no one
peers beneath but you who know
one day your body will be ripe,
ready for northern cities, the dance

where you wear purple ribbons
curling in your hair as you
shed dusty skin behind footlights
and stretch toward one sweet note.

this is everything i did not want to feel*
(in the voice of Mary Wollstonecraft 1759-1797)
by Grace Cavalieri

I wanted rest from running, from asking for love,
Bitter lips tasted, lips lost,
Breaking teeth into my mouth.

I wanted, before the sun came up,
To pray: *Thank You for*
The day, for Nature advancing its tender mercies.

I wanted a crescendo of women
Saying: *There is enough for all ...*
We will walk through the dark of this house.
Words will seep through the walls. We are able.
There is a light on the hill we can walk through.

Women everywhere are aching.

I would preach a ballad from the roof,
Sing to mermaids and children,
Cross limbs with scholars,
Leave footprints in the snow,
Write the weeds of our history,
Bring our pieces together. That is what I wanted.

Why these crowds rising in clusters against me,
This sun setting in its sky sending
A bloody cloth as a letter of love.

  * Special Featured Poem by permission of the author and Jacaranda Press.

frida paints her portrait looking in a mirror
by Don Cellini

          Night is falling
            all alone
              I am
            faraway
         in the house
         in Coyocán
     there is no breeze
      there is no moon
           tonight
        where are you

              Diego

        where are you
           tonight
      there is no moon
     there is no breeze
        in Coyoacán
         in the house
           faraway
              I am
             alone
      night is falling.

Looking in a mirror
Frida paints her portrait

what borges told me
by Don Cellini

In the Cervantes Museum
at 85 Atocha Street
in Madrid

on the second floor
in a glass case
in the exhibit area

is a quill pen
used by the famous author
to write *Don Quixote*.

Borges insisted
that the pen
knew Cervantes well,

the emotions that run through the adventures
the increased heartbeat
that came with the name Dulcinea.

Borges, if this is true, tell me
what does my laptop
know about me?

He didn't answer,
didn't say a word.
Borges didn't tell me anything.

starkweather: june 25, 1959
by Christopher Conlon

the stranger   he wrote   near the end
to his mother   in a poem   *asks no greater glory*
till life   *is through*   *than to spend*
one last minute   *in wilderness*
and he had   that minute   (though less
than a minute)   at the end   just past
midnight   walking shackled from

```
         prison hospital to     death chamber        100 yards
           gray walls     beside him    gray guard towers    above
             faceless men        around him      gray pavement
           beneath     (avoiding cracks saving      mother's back)
              but there    to his left    sheeted with light
                 was grass     palegray     nearly white
                    in the fluorescent     sheen         smooth
                  as a buzzcut      yet growing         sprouting
                     bursting the innards       of the earth
                  and he pictured     himself         diving into
                      it     rolling in     it    tearing out
                   clumps shouting     in joy          inhaling
                     them      eating      them      opening
                    arms to         night sky to         moon to
                   Nebraska wind     one last minute
                    in wilderness      and he felt love
                 for everyone then    everything    for Mother for
                    Caril for     black-capped chickadees and
                      love he felt       such love     love
                    as he'd never felt     love        O Love!
```

in the absence of knowing
after Louise Glück
by Nina Corwin

The ocean waves won't tell.
And likewise, the trees don't speak our language.
They just rustle softly in the night.

And so we turn to you,
Oh, Great Celestial Psychoanalyst

hoping you'll put it all together:
A plus B equals C, something more conclusive
than "I think, therefore I am."

But silently, just out of view
from behind the fainting couch

peeking out of bushes, allegedly
from deserts
or mountaintops too craggy to access

your occasional grunts and inscrutable nods
are infinitely open to interpretation.

Looking skyward we lie, couch-bound,
and wait for answers.
Absent that, we project our own:

You are the scowling father, punishing
father, the loving father we never had.

And we spill out our fears and transferential
longings, our most
precious resentments, serve up our sins

in a great buffet of contrition
waiting for your pronouncement.

For you to say
something. Anything to make sense
of this earthly mess.

the fluorescent range funeral home
by Jim Curran

Pale complexion under milk-gray
Sky before dark, still as evening's
Soul on birch bark mound
Earth's florescent radiance, spectre
Spotlight, haunting memory of
Feathered hey neh, heh neh song
Wafting o'er flame Great Spirit
Kack Kack, "kte", spirit rises
As Anguta fills his canoe
May I be fed from the bowl in the ghost lodge
May my ashes rise to dance around the moon
May I meet the girls who make love to the stars
May Breathmaker show me the way
May I not feel the gods, as did Coyote
May I ride in Gluskac's canoe when he returns
May I return to be nurtured by Nokomis
Holy stories to be told of those
Who rose to learn of the secrets
And returned to fill the hearts of
My children

the boar tracks fading
by G. L. Curtis

Inside the barn, the smell of horse
Bridle bits, and harness traces

Hang urgent on the wall.

A dog lies on the flattened straw
Its belly couched in fear;
Its body motionless like a forgotten roar.

The geese attack in groups.
Their long necks nod in unison.

Outside, milk buckets rattle in the hand
Like ancient censers; the air
Is filled with the sweet odour of cow.

All part, for down the cobbled path
A figure moves, swaying evil-eyed
Like a crippled king.

The geese attack in groups.
Their long necks nod in unison.

>   A child trips
>   Runs
>   Trips again
>   Runs
>   Trips again
>   Runs.

I remember now
Moving into age;
The dog-fear dumb in the barn;
The boar tracks fading.

proper geometry
by Jill Darling

a.

it was as she said a circumstance of touch
we touched

brushed
at the end of the day.
the (square) root of a side a, how to get to hypotenuse.
each small circle has its own radius.
each triangle reflected or remembered.
each figure represents sums as yet unfolded.
please report all charted percentages here.

b.

at four o'clock the experts will play jazz.
and we will each wear our genders in anticipation of the unquestionable
social questions.
trace the circle or the square root of its circumference. look no further.
that is, if you have radio frequency—tune in—listen for the notes
performed on every personal level.
have we entered the hypotenuse region?
calculate the area as yet undetermined.
jazz this.
love that.
the diameter might recall (350 times X) or the color of a circle
on a monday.
pink ink.
an overall sense of shaded and gendered colors.
we play notes.
the fraction represents the probability of acquaintance.
the ratio of.
green to green—depending on days of the week.
draw this pink like—attach it to the proper rectangle.
divide the cube into.

c.

write letters to everyone you know informing them of the mathematical
changes at hand.
they will be impressed.
they will create compatible lists and shapes.
the solutions will be pleasing.

false starts for cursed letters
by Mitchell L. H. Douglas

At the grocery,
found a losing lottery ticket
at the bottom of my basket—

a bad luck sign
if I ever saw one...

      †

    I am
the bite from your morning
apple, skin removed, the pulp
browning in air.

      †

    Can I be something other
than pieces?

      †

Bed unmade for two days,
better this way I tell myself.
Tried to burn your number,
but flame won't make it fade.

      †

    I am
the mark that wraps your finger,
skin's record of days, reminder
of the ring, removed.

      †

    Can I be something
other than missing?

mister on the angels
by Jim Elledge

Every angel is terrible, he
told Mister. Mister agrees. He found one
dancing a striptease on his martini
glass, one on his pillow sparkling and clean,
one in his medicine chest mirror who
blew him kisses. He's forgotten the rest
though he described each in a notebook so
he could recall their faces, but it's lost.

Terrible all right because their beauty
isn't theirs—nor their breath, nor their steps here
to there; because, stepping out of a frieze
of stars, they bring word—sword-sharp and bright—
no one wants or even gets 'til it's clear
that it's too late for mercy or for flight.

napoleon
by J. Glenn Evans

In Seattle I sit and watch the rain
Wash down upon the city's core
And I think of you on that rock, St. Helena
Looking out the window at the rain

I've read your diary and notes on glory
Were those your real thoughts, or just PR?
You could have been a Cromwell of Europe
Set the stage for a true democracy

What if you had made the rule of France
Exemplary of how best to rule
For the benefit of all the people
Would citizens then have cause to burn castles?

You'd had your glory without cannon
We might know the names of those who died
Those who perished in the Russian snow
Those who fought for you and against you

Did you give a thought to all the men
Who perished in the Russian snow
The van Goghs, the Poes, the Picassos,
Whose names we shall never know

You sit on the rock of St. Helena and gaze at the rain
That cleaned their wounds and drained away their hopes
The same rain that now falls on Seattle
Rain reminds me of other lives lost for glory

on the road to el paso
by Manuel Figuroa

On the road to El Paso, all alone,
Hours to go before reaching Socorro,
My head nods. All at once I jerk awake.
There: A battered pickup full of sorrow,
Pocked with designs of dirt.
There, on that sun-scorched skirt,

There's a pale, thin man standing by his truck,
Stained hat blueing lines in his sun-baked face,
Aged slate overalls weightless on his frame.
I stop. "Can I take you out of this place?"
"Nope," he says, "Truck's no good.
"Can't fix it. Wish I could.

"I'll just wait for some po-leece man to come."
Six frail ragged children all streaked with grime
Huddle together under the truck's shade.
Inside, there's a woman long past her prime.
As she steps down, her skirt—
Hand-sewn—touches the dirt.

And even in this stifling heat she drapes
Over her thin shoulders an ancient shawl.
It is she who takes the oldest child's hand,
She who leads him, a slim boy, not too tall,
To stand mute before me.
At last she says, "This be

"My first-born, a good boy, hard-working, brave.
"But," she jerks her head at her gaunt children,
"There ain't no money, ain't no food for them."
The boy speaks up. "I can work. I'm thirteen."
Her eyes caress my face.
"Please Mister, make a place

"For him in your car. Take him off with you."
"She whispers, "He will grow. He'll do you fine."
I turn my back. The few steps to my car
Feel caught in a mire of unmoving time.
I flee to El Paso,
For what else could I do?

My eyes sting with tears as I seek
The mirrored image: reflection—

Warped with dust—of that fragile boy
Lost in waves of desolation.

there / here
by Steven Finch

The word "there" means everywhere but here,
    but "here" we also know what's happening there:
the attack on the World Trade Center's twin
    towers in New York; the continuing attacks on
Afghanistan; the attacks on African countries
    and Iraq; and, the other day, the blood bath
in four full train stations in Madrid, Spain—
    the city where I spent some of my wildest days
one year after its firm dictator had finally died;
    the country from which my lover comes,
my *pareja* who's watching dish television
    and who tells me after a walk with the dog
that Israel has just killed Sheikh Ahmad Yassin,
    venerable blind old man and religious leader,
in Gaza, in Palestine (an ill-defined territory,
    the biblical Holy Land, also called Canaan,
a state illegally occupied, withdrawn from,
    occupied again, and now walled... in or out?),
with two bodyguards while the three men were
    leaving a mosque after morning prayers.
News on Spanish TV quickly moves on
    to the capturing of the suspected culprits
of the bombing of the Madrid train stations.
    Moved, we light a candle and put it outside,
something that we and many other people did
    for the twin towers, Afghanistan, Iraq.
And here, in the twenty-first century A.D.,
    in this country that's supposed to be neutral
but really never has been and never will be,
    here, my heart is working like a walkman
that has skip protection yet keeps repeating
    Kyle Eastwood and Diane King's cover of
T. Thomas's *Why Can't We Live Together*,
    music and lyrics and an explosive voice
that spread throughout this old house
    and should somehow spread and reach
and fill ears and hearts and minds and
    be fully understood by everybody still alive
from here to there and everywhere between.

undocumented
by Maureen Tolman Flannery

They walk for days in the desert
beat down upon by the heat of a hostile sun
by the wants of a wife left behind,
by a child's disease
by the needs of a mother who feeds them all
and eats only at her own oversized heart.
The balls of their feet are one thick oozing blister.

And some of them die of sadness
huddled against each other
against the cold of a desert night,
their backs full of cactus spurs
as if each one were San Sebastian.

As they near the high fence
they fear the helicopter's search light,
the signs they cannot read.
They fear the stranger and the compatriot,
the night and the day,
the *coyote* they have paid a family's life savings
to keep them safe,
the guns of the border guards
and the thunder in their ears
of their own fragile hearts drumming
like *tambores* of the festival dancers back home.

Hope and hunger swirl into a tailwind
sweeping them north toward the border.
Desperation drives them over;
the INS sends them back much faster.

When it comes against the edge
which deed, I wonder,
should be the honored claim,
or should it be need?
And how many must die for a chance
at what those who have it
don't even want?
And what, then, is the bottom line,
and who has crossed it?

my father typing
by Gretchen Fletcher

The portable Royal's keys clacked
on the back porch
where my father sat shirtless,
sweat running in rivulets down his chest
and beading on blonde hairs around his nipples
as he agonized over each word
he would deliver the following Sunday
from the pulpit – words pounded out
with two-fingered efficiency –
fingers whose clean short nails I can see
twenty years after his death
- They say one's nails continue to grow –
I put the picture from my mind
to see him as he was when
I came home from school.

"Shhh," my mother says.
"He's writing his sermon." I go
behind the walls of my own room
where I wish he were
saying all those words to me.

don't mourn. organize!
by H. Susan Freireich

One by one
the pieces of my heart,
mind and body—
I can't speak for the soul—
fall back into place
as I let go
of longing for things
beyond my control.
"Focus on the task
at hand. Keep busy,"
my father, the doctor, says.
It is his prescription
for life,
and he has come back
from the dead
to take my hand
and remind me

of all that is good
in me
and the world.

ivana, the queen of prague
by Mary L. Gardner

She walks
As if meeting her Lord,
Who will take her to bed
Shouting, "Glory!"

Her face
Has begun its slow melting,
A pool of liquid was
Reforming.

In her fur,
From before all the wars,
One hears the brown voices
Rejoicing.

Her children, now grown,
Whisper stories about her,
Then, shaking their heads,
Travel homeward.

In St. Wenceslas Square
On Jan Palach Day,
Police hoses froze her
To silver.

"Your name?" yelled the guard.
She looked past his shoulder,
Swept her arms round the buildings,
Embraced them.

The fog of Prague
Is a scarf at her throat,
Her long hair a helmet
For freedom.

From the old bridge,
Her hands hold her city.
Behind her, the rusty sound
Of statues bowing.

gift
by Bernadette Geyer

He gave her a gift
of stones.
Hefty, weighted
with the love
of a whole history
of earth.
Solid, smooth,
pocked with age.
Each stone
she collected like years,
the years
she collected like gifts,
each holding her feet
to earth, holding
earth to her feet.
Dimpled, marbled,
timeless.
Solid, smooth,
pregnant with meaning.
He gave her meaning,
a gift of stones.

where the *air is beyond happiness*
by John Gilgun

One September morning before sunrise
in a place where *the air is beyond happiness*,
as Ben writes, I stared down at a ceramic mask

I'd made and its eyes, which were closed,
opened suddenly and I saw a mountain road
lined with aspen trees golden in the falling snow,

and in the center of the road I saw a mirror
which was also a river reflecting clouds illuminated
by a peculiar moon shaped like a black-billed magpie,

whose eyes, which were open, closed suddenly,
revealing Mayan glyphs on its bluish-green eyelids,
glyphs carved by Rabbit God on the first day of the world.

the letting go
by Robert L. Giron

You want out to smell the grass,
trying to head nature but can't,
drained like a beached whale pup
you collapse, panting.
Then as if the high priest
I apply holy oil,
the last rites.
Your eyes said it all,
crystals to my very core,
you gave me a glimpse into myself,
a razor against soft skin.
Later like Popocatepetl,
suppressed, I explode, seeing
the faces of Woody and Grandma
vivid as the day they left,
lava flowed without control.
—Woody barely moved as I washed
his hands after nature's call,
as he pushed the airport wheel chair
closer to the basin sink.
I knew then I would never
see him again and so
his last words: "Mother, I
think I'm going to die"
were his last before landing
at Dallas, that fateful place.—
Then praying, chanting
like a shaman, I led Grandma
to her rest.
Exhausted, I fell asleep only
to be awaken by the nurse's:
"Sorry, she's gone."
—So when you looked back
toward the backseat, excited
to be in the front seat,
your eyes troubled me.
They cast innocence seen by mothers
knowing their naked children would be gassed.
At the vet's you collapsed on the
hard, cool floor—we, attentive
not wanting to alarm, held back,
slowly caressing you.
Then the sparkle glossed over—
a star folding into itself,

a moment became infinity—
your head fell and with it our joy.

that bitch-goddess
"So then, when you'd got your hands on the
girl, did you take turns at balling her,
seeing that she liked swapping husbands?"— Euripides
by Paula Goldman

You weren't carried off on Paris' back like the blond,
    blue-eyed babe in Gozzoli's *The Rape of Helen*, looking

wistfully back at a house full of guests. Good looks attract
    good looks and you were taken with Paris' curly locks,

golden Oriental robes. Paris was ambrosia after a steady
    diet of Spartan fish and lamb. And yet you said of

Aphrodite, it was that bitch who caused you to leave your
    husband's bed for twenty years. Even you admitted

Menelaus wasn't short on brains or fine body parts. So why
    blame good looks for your unhappiness? I look

between the covers of fashion magazines and see women
    standing, looking mean, reaching their hands into

tight jeans. "Princess, pearl of kings," what was it like
    to pass from a stately king to a young prince, then to

his brother, before Menelaus fetched you? How fast you were
    to forget how sweet your husband was just after

Hermione came, *she was only a girl*, feeding your ravenous,
    but small, pink mouth, black grapes and honeyed

treats. The women in the magazines have their hair whipped
    by wind or slicked by gel; their otherwise depilated

bodies shine off the page. Tall in your long gown, in your
    silver cloak, "enticing Helen," what did you feel

when middle-age crept over your liquid ramparts, when a
    little belly shook as you walked? Did you agonize

that Paris might run around, looking for a younger crowd,
>   did you want him to, tiring of his perfumed skin,

banal compliments? Then would you imagine Menelaus' fair-
>   haired body against your still lithe limbs? The women

in the fashion ads will grow old, too, but not in public
>   view. Enfolded in a shining robe, hoping beauty

would save you, and it did, Helen, thinking of your own skin,
>   you did what any mortal would do: you covered your

pearly ass. You said it was a phantom who went with Paris
>   while you stayed in Egypt and took hot baths. *All*

women are not Helen . . . but have Helen in their hearts. I look
>   for you in the ads, on the movie screen, in dressing

room mirrors. How often it takes a Paris and a beauty
>   contest to make Eros surface on a dolphin's back.

lyrics
for Ferron, for Joan Armatrading, for Janis Ian (2004)
by Jewelle Gomez

There is an edge
your voice
drops over
becoming sand
infinite particles
distinct and indistinguishable
shifting beneath me.

Not melody or motion
sound or muscle
but you
sifting down
hourglass or wind
until you are concrete

Only then the words
wrap around
and open
against my skin—
moths fluttering dust.
I gasp

sound seeps in
bonding with the
pulse of blood inside.
Improbable pairings
conclude in places I
never expected to be
or be seen.

A song set out
net or kite or
parable
a mist in the air
I breathe.

running home from school *
for Molly and Daisy and
for Gracie, the one who was recaptured (2004)
by Jewelle Gomez

In the story there are three small girls
dark smudges on the landscape
streaking past squat eucalyptus away from
a thief who has stolen their lives.

Small, smaller, smallest
in too big shoes under hard sun,
crossing cracked earth like rabbits
chasing rain.

They stay steps ahead of trackers
who would return them to the box
meant to shape their future into
maids, cooks and minders
of other people's children.

They are more at ease on the land
than in the barracks they've fled—
rough chemise, tin plate of food, 'protectors' faces
pinched with assurance they know what
a race needs—extinction.

Jigalong sounds like a playground in a children's book
and it was until the men came in cars to protect them
from themselves. Save them from blackness they said,
sweeping young faces into cages for more than half a century.
Mothers left behind with only the magic of waiting.

On the road the girls sleep in the shade of a myrtle tree
hoping to dream a way through the bush, leaving
no scent or footprints to betray their guess
about which is the road toward home.
They sleep to dream a way out of captivity
to learn to fly.

A wire wall spans the land
from here to there, longest
structure on the continent—
Rabbit-proof fence to keep the pests
from hindering colonial progress.
The girls dream it as a finger drawn
across the rocks and scrub brush
pointing the way.

From a distance they are so like us—
small on an unknown landscape
pushing against the container,
following a landmark we've never seen fully.

There's too much to take in all at once
but each post and timber is a sign
crossing a thousand miles, made longer
by the smallness of their feet.
Like putting an ear to the railroad track,
feeling the fence sends the sound of a
family dreaming their return.

Following the fence to Jigalong, to the magic waiting,
three small girls steal themselves home.

* In response to the film *The Rabbit-Proof Fence* which told the true story of mixed race, Aborigine children stolen from their homes in Australia by the government for more than 70 years, a practice that only ended in 1971.

poem for the brother you never had
by John Grey

You're out there
on a rock somewhere,
imagining the brother
that might have been.
There was no abortion,

no miscarriage,
just the rock with you on it,
the water splashing its gray sides.

They were too poor for another kid,
too poor to do anything
but lead you to this river,
he to show you how to fish,
she with solemn instructions
on the stripping of the scales.

But maybe there was a brother
and he taught you
to walk out into the stream,
to ignore the tug on your legs,
the dampness of your jeans.
He said, sit on the rock
and I'll be by for you.
And all the time nothing but the water lapping,
a constant senseless sound,
like the brother you never had
speaking to the brother you never were.

holding hands
by Benjamin Scott Grossberg

I was eighteen watching a movie with other students in a dorm room
the first time a man held my hand. His name was Shawn.
He wore large yellow Mickey Mouse slippers and perfectly round
wire rims; his hair was jet black with a bleached forelock.

Someone shut the lights; someone else flipped on the VCR; both
a pipe and lighter were passed around. And then Shawn, who had

seated himself on the floor next to me, reached down and intertwined
my fingers in his. The movie, Disney, I think, seemed long—
very long, incredibly long, even—because of course as soon as
Shawn touched me I became instantly, completely, manifestly

excited. Thankfully the room was dark. I didn't know Shawn.
Not well. And I wasn't attracted to him. But no man had ever

touched me, not in that way before. I gave no sign of pleasure. In fact,
neither Shawn nor I acknowledged that we were holding hands—
not throughout the entire film, no turn, no shy smile, no movement
of any sort. We both studiously stared at the television screen

as if we were going to be tested on it afterwards. Still I was fixated:
each of his fingers felt particular, erotic, slightly lubricated

by sweat, like an independent sensory organ. Each felt hot
and disturbingly organic. And the whole time others were around,
passing the pipe, making cracks at the screen. None of them
seemed to be aware. Was this a scandal of human sexuality,

this semi-public arousal? Was it better because they were there?
Months passed before Shawn and I felt brave enough to kiss,

and even then, some time longer before we'd wake up, sprawled
across each other, before we wasted entire college days
stuck to our dorm room beds as to fly paper, and months after that
before it ended—as it had to, strange German art house

looking boy I was never attracted to—but none of it, none of it
lasted as long as that movie, the name of which I can't remember,

the eternity I sat as still as possible in the dark, thankful
under a long t-shirt. There was love after, with other men,
and sex after, with him, but it never seemed to last those eternities,
and it never—is this possible?—seemed to feel so good.

eyes of wax
by JoseMarGuerr

The opinions of dogs
are not as important
as my own
and to listen to mine
was your pleasure.
You drank them down
like cold milk in a glass.

These days when
I speak to you,
your eyes open
like common flowers.
They don't shine with color or
change with understanding.
They don't blink, or answer me.
Your eyes are dead rainbows.
They only stare like worlds of wax
imprisoned in sockets of stone.

letter of denunciation
by Piotr Gwiazda

Dear Chief Investigator:

This is not my first letter of denunciation.
Remember Queen of Diamonds? And the poisoned jelly,
and the man with false teeth, and the light-bulb swindler,
and the bug that made you sick— that was me,
I exposed them! Why, out of a sense of duty . . .
If only it's a matter of national security,
I'm always at your service. The post office hates me.
Sometimes I also call, always from a pay phone.

And I could tell you stories: where life is simple
like two plus two, where dreams always come true
like the horoscope or weather forecast,
the informer assembles his magnum opus.
He improvises a little, drinks an inch of whisky,
books put him to sleep, TV makes him dizzy,
a gun on his table, a cat guards his house . . .
But time is running out and I have things to tell you

about the man whose name I cannot mention.
He counts his fingers, looks through binoculars.
He sits on a park bench, sending data.
And now he's leaving the police headquarters,
which you must search, but mind you do it fast
for I am the explosive, I am the bomb,
I am the ticking clock. Now please come save me.

the choice
by Piotr Gwiazda

Say Yes, soon all misgivings will be gone.
A submarine shifts in the Baltic Sea.
Say No, tomorrow you will sleep alone.

If you can bring a statue back to stone,
If you can put a gun next to your knee,
Say Yes, soon all misgivings will be gone.

You tremble picking up the telephone,
You have been taken hostage by TV;
Say No, tomorrow you will sleep alone.

There is no honor that you haven't won,
No country where you'd rather want to be;
Say Yes, soon all misgivings will be gone.

But caught in dialectic's danger zone,
You wish the choices weren't two but three
(Say No, tomorrow you will sleep alone)—

For neither one can be depended on.
Lock your door always with a different key . . .
Say Yes, soon all misgivings will be gone.
Say No, tomorrow you will sleep alone.

on a bench: my life
by Myronn Hardy

How did I believe life would change?

My choices so limited I had to conjure
something that reflected light. It's cold
in Venezia but I sleep on a bench
the sea will soon swallow.

Here in a small jacket I'm observed by a poet
wayward in his search for a canal through this mind.

Ethiopia.

Yes.

I'm from Addis Ababa. Family slaughtered by
a murder of ghosts. Some were visible with guns
others inside skin   arms   fingers   proud
lives were all they knew. This place
of cathedrals   Catholic saints but bodies
are still nailed down   carried through crowds.

Return.

Yes.

To the desert lush as cantos.
The green place where we shared bread is
all I need: my sister spinning about the room   dinner

of roasted fish   yellow lentils as my father
tells of his favorite student   my uncle in church
speaking Ge'ez.

We have prayed so many years.
We are scrolls tightly wound yet I'm the only one left.

Return.

Yes.

In this head is all I have. My warm-poor
country these feet will never touch. I hope the water I
cup   let go   will spill over my desolate land.

the last world of fire and trash
by Joy Harjo

I don't know anything anymore
or if that cricket is still singing
in a country where crickets are banned.

I'm Indian in a strange pastiche of hurt and rain
smells like curry and sweat
from a sunset rock and roll restaurant.
A familiar demon groaning with fear
has stalked me here, ruins poetry, then
his swollen pride commandeers.

Beneath the moon rocking above Los Angeles
or outside the stomp dance fire of memory,
I told him, you can choose to hate me
for going too far, or for being a nothing
next to a pretty nothing like you.

So long, goodbye, oh fearful one.
My desires had turned into a small mountain.
Of dirty clothes, sax gig bag, guitar
books, shoes and grief
that I packed and carried
from one raw wound to another.

I can't get betrayal out of my heart,
out of my mind
in this hotel room where I'm packing for home.
I've seen that same face whirring

in the blur of a glass of wine
after the crashed dance,
the goodbye song
in the last world of fire and trash.

The most dangerous demons spring from fire
and a broken heart, smell of bittersweet aftershave
and the musk of a thousand angels.
And then I let that thought go running away
because I refuse to stay in bondage
to an enemy, who thinks he wants what I have.

I turned my cheek as my head parted through a curtain of truth
and erupted from the spirit world to this gambling place—
And I send prayers skyward
on smoke.
Hvsaketvmese, Hvsaketvmese.
Release this suffering.
May the pretty beast and all the world know peace.

I refuse to sum it up anymore; it's not possible.
I give it up
to the battering of songs against the light,
to the singing of the earnest cricket
in the last world of fire and trash.

navigating the warning
for Reggie
by Joy Harjo

From eternity to never is a river
Of renegade stars
Home-starved planets
Past the stream of thinking-without-direction:
That's where it comes from—
You'll have no exact address in the mess of humanness
And go down in the punch of red history and earthly cowboys.
The body is a helix
Of the dreams of ancestors
Cultivate the wisdom here, in molecular funk and grease
Navigate swiftly
Beyond the scurry of the mind having a drink
With friends at the café
Beyond the limb of knowledge thick with crows

Perched on a broken overhang
Over crashing fresh waters,
Beyond time.

reality show
by Joy Harjo

Nizhoniigo * no hey nay
Nizhoniigo no hey wa ney
Nizhoniigo no hey nay
Nizhoniigo no hey wa ney

How do we get out of here?
Smoke hole crowded with too much thinking
Too many seers
And prophets of prosperity
We call it real, we call it real

What are we doing in this mess of forgetfulness?
Ruled by sharp things, baby girls in stiletto heels
Beloved ones doing street time
We call it real

What are we doing napping, through war?
We've lost our place of in the order of kindness
Children are killing children
We call it real, we call it real.

What are we doing forgetting love?
Under mountains of trash, a river on fire
We can't be bought, forced or destroyed.
Just what is real?

Nizhoniigo no hey nay
Nizhoniigo no hey wa ney
Nizhoniigo no hey nay
Nizhoniigo no hey wa ney

* Nizhoniigo: Navajo (or Dineh) which means beautiful within and without

after-dinner remarks
(after dinner with guillermo gomez-pena and the sisters)
by suzan shown harjo

we are uncommon peoples with much in common
                              for starters, mutual oppression

we are not the half-time show
        for the whiteman's redskins game
        or his taco-bell-selling chihuahua
        we do not resemble
        frito bandito or chief wahoo

we are not the pastoral peons
        of the americas
        or the idiot children
        of juan valdez and
        the indian butter maiden

we get the same sleazy propositions
        from california, chiapas
        and washington
        and all the states
        of mind-control

we catch the same nafta nasties
        and gatt gnats
        from sleeping
        with too many dogs
        and fleas

we speak the language of the heart
        but with europese in between

do they really think we cannot recognize ourselves
        just because they shot out some windows and mirrors

we have our own borders to cross and crosses to bear
        and that is family business

we are related by blood
        by red hands and red dirt
        by blood of the sun
        by blood on the streets
        by blood on the feet of lives on the run

we have toasts to make
            with sangria
            and that is thicker than wine

in sangria   to mexico, the u.s. and all the rest:
                    you are the documented illegal aliens
                    never forget, you still are guests
                    in our red quarter of Mother Earth

aria
by Daniel Hefko

The blind, old woman's cane
tat—tattles on the cobbled stones
of Via Speziali, and the infant morning air
swallows whole each vagrant note
thirstily as Romulus and Remus
suckling on a she-wolf.
No sound's too small or fugitive
to escape air's thrift
as it composes morning.
With every stride
she seems a statue
stepping out of stone, moving
free and captive
between worlds.
            In the way that mold
knows where to find old bread, she turns
and disappears into a *tabaccheria*.
Moments later she stops outside the shop,
lights a cigarette, then breathes in
and out what she can't see. Walking back to where
she came from, for an instant there is nothing
underneath her cane but air. She begins
to fall, then doesn't, then walks until she's gone.
All this time, I'm standing
in the middle of the street, and as soon
as she is out of sight, a melody
builds and fills the hole
inside my head
where she has gone. It doesn't stop
with me. It moves
through shapes
of things, through things
that I can't see.

anima
by Wendy Hilsen-Bernard

Like a rain full of promise
after a season of drought
She waters our parched places,
Her revivifying elixir
restoring glory
and gladness.
The ultimate alchemist
She works her magic
with passion's fire
Her white-hot tongue
consuming all that is false
leaving us
only the gold brilliance
of our Truth
leaving us
dazzled and dazzling.
The consummate musician
She plays her song
in all that shines with beauty
in all that sings nature's grace.
As for me
I like the volume
turned up,
turned on
by
Her amazing ways
as I gaze intently
to see
how She animates
each object
each being
lighting them
igniting them
exciting me
inviting me in
so
my eyes - can see their shining
my heart - can feel their pain
my ears- can hear their song
my soul can dance with them
to the music of the ages.
Yo! Saint Francis,
Make me an instrument too.

june 15
(from
As Experience)
by Laura Hinton

You again, impossible to miss the landscape   razor-edged with ripped map
you follow its broken backbone   the sage of the Sierra   a sleeping roll cauldron
caught fire

two men lather up in a desert horse pool

The chevy was marked with a licorice flavor   black, black, the psychic
would say: pass on any density   in any cloud, every eye lifts in the haze of
cigarettes and false lighting   the fire stewed a rolling tundra   half off
the land, the black car with the scull ran into deep cobalt veins   those passages
come away with their own specific narratives   tumbled down in bottles
of broken colored glass in the desert in the breakdown of a metal cap
we found a scrap   but the sympathetic nerve was tired out

terror travels
by Walter Holland

It's a miracle that anyone travels. They can see inside your shoe
and examine the trifling incidentals you carry on you.

Iris, finger, teeth. Identity seems complete. Why bother with a name
when family trees need never be explained? One cotton swab and all
those shaky

ancestors will spill their mix of pedigree, starting with headman Adam
down to incendiary Eve.

louisiana
by Peter Huggins

The sky is different there.
Stretched thin, it is
An expanse so distant
That I have gotten lost in it.

In Alabama the sky is warm,
Intimate, a welcome embrace.
It is a kiss on the lips,
A caress of cheek and bone.

I do not know where the sky
Changes: perhaps the change
Occurs on the Mississippi coast,
The old Spanish West Florida,

The shadows of the conquistadores
Stretching across Bay St. Louis.
I could ask the pelicans—
They know everything and are

Not shy about saying so.
I could consult the paintings
Of Walter Anderson but I would
Probably get lost in them, too.

No, the change is in the water.
When you cross the Pearl River
Into Louisiana, you
Can see the sky for yourself.

route 501 south
by Lucas Jacob

The road is empty. On the radio
the correspondent's voice cracks with distance
from the North Pole. Each word brings insistence:
the world does stretch on, to the end, in snow.

Motion is frozen here, she says. The waves
have been stilled and painted white—sugared wisps
of meringue forever held before my lips.
Her figures are the only ones I have.

I think of the Pole, imagine such weather,
such blurring of day and night. Later, I will
miss this voice, like my lover, like the chills
up my spine when we wintered together.

Fogging up car windows, every breath seems
to ask why, each day, we go to extremes.

acapulco
by John Jenkison

He barters marijuana on the beach
where a child-high concrete culvert gags

its ceaseless sewage into the postcard bay.
By sunset he's rococo, high in a third floor

walk-up and veering into his rippled mirror,
closely shaved and massaging a pancake finish

over his baby-butterfly cheek. Nettlesome
penis folded into the nylon fist

of his pantyhose, he conjures a face of mascara,
liner and rouge. *Ya, soy Selena.*

And you must be a tourist, nature's briefest
pinprick of light, in rhyme with the fishermen's lamps

floating the black harbor in constellations—
a star so infinitely distant that you

count the years in photons. One cigarette
follows another up the hillside's raucous

streets, where the neon flicker of old beer signs
buzzes in your blood. Behind you, tides

drum the wet rocks in an iodine flood.
Greeting you politely at the bar,

a boy in epaulettes ushers you to a stage-side
table for two where you sit alone with your troubles.

You order a drink made famous in Havana.
Selena whispers a torch song into the microphone's

mesh, snaps her paste-on lashes, lurid
castanets against your tom-tom eyes.

She splashes your cheek with Revlon *Moonbeam* lips.
Later, she drinks a hole in your credit card.

You noodle your hand to her shaved thigh's limit,
but she spits you into the tire-worn street where salt

in the coastal air mixes a paste in your throat,
and yellow-ribbed mongrels slink in the alley mouths.

Mexican boys in *maquiladora* miracle-bras—
latter-day pirates in eye-shadow deep as a gringo's

blues, who brassily parrot their sisters, plunder
their timbre, their nylons, their gestures, their blonde synthetic

second-hand wigs—flex at the hips as you drift
like a merchant sloop aching for boarders; each man

walks his personal plank to the ebbing sea.

death food
by Fran Jordan

Cars from out-of-state signal something wrong.
Friends and neighbors offer food
to fill the emptiness death served this family.

Mostly untouched, it overflows
the dining room table, cupboards,
fridge and kitchen countertops.
Fried chicken: whole plates of it.
Bowls of salads. Jell-O molds.
Anything that can be chopped or shaped
into a semblance of food.
Three angel food cakes,
one with little strawberries
drawn in icing on the top.

We move silently among these mountains,
winding through the valleys of death food.
Sipping bourbon or iced tea,
we take our liquids in shades of amber.

I wander through the house, collecting stray glasses
to wash and dry, wash and dry.
"Where is my glass?" my mother asks.
"I don't seem able to keep track of it."
I'd washed it, of course,
trying to restore order
to the chaos of this house
with all its food and people,
trying to rinse away my grief.

temazcal *
by Claire Joysmith

naked in time
sweat coating my skin
darkness swathing my eyes

once embers have
danced the universe
away my hair flares
i lose my halo flung
into the night

i burn tears
croak into
name-singing
eagle words
turning into
ancient gods
life-death
one

we rattle
strange rhythms
drum-drum-drum
yearning into
warrior prayer
plexus powered
to a sunglow

refugees in a clay urn
we welcome long-
lost chants:

> *pájaro de fuego*
> *cenzontle de aire*
> *palo de lluvia*
> *barro que canta*
> *espiral de copal*
> *plegaria infinita***

---

*   Traditional Mexican sweat-lodge.
**   firebird/ airborne mockingbird/ rainstick/ singing clay/ copal spiral/ infinite petition

my jar of leeches
by Jacqueline Jules

Ancient doctors entered
anxious homes bringing leeches
as the best cure for fever.
Good minds fooled for centuries;
siphoning the right body fluid
in the wrong direction.
Imagine a doctor in 1818
with thinning hair
and sagging eyes, seated
at a wooden table, judging
his life by a jar of leeches.
Three-inch black worms
wiggling in water. A lifetime
fighting death by draining
the source of strength.
The decisions of each decade
could be discounted in the next.
As the years flow faster and faster
like a gushing red wound,
I consider my history
and wonder what
will prove to be
my jar of leeches.

this time of sand and teeth
(Make Peace Not War)
by Gunilla Theander Kester

At this time of sand and teeth
we sink to our knees, crushed like grapes,
ground like corn, crumbled like strong buildings.

I think of how to forget the tone
of our dreams and songs in the morning,
our prayers and dreams at night.

I wonder how we will remember
the pace and the paths up the warlike mountain,
the tracks and the tales of those who return.

They come back—wild eyes, burnt skin—
with voices like so many fires in the dark,
not knowing how to paint the source of the light they have seen.

We know that Isaac must have wept
and kept a fear of knives along with his heart, that
the sound of angels made him shimmer like snow.

There are those who feel at home on the Masada
and there are those who choose to stay in the homeless camps below;
both must learn to love and use the weapons we now hold.

On the top of the mountain, myths are born, heroes and war cries
down below babies are born and mothers who will steal for food
while those who get hurt howl in pain.

The world is whole and it is breaking—
their pain, our pain—who can name the difference
when all the pieces of the world are ours to embrace.

pennies in a cracked cup
by Peter Klappert

               Faded red and blue borders
    on airmail envelopes, and other envelopes
with the corners gone . splayed shoe boxes, slides
       and black-and-white snapshots, negatives
           starting to fox
in their glassine sleeves . pottery shards, shards of
     busted family, a tiny
           black birdhead, obsidian,
    nearly transparent, found
on a vanished lakeshore in the
        desert outside El Paso .
         old college texts
–chemistry, anatomy, psychology– their
     ridiculous underlining . lint,
         two dimes and a nickel, someone's
    shattered black comb and
a cryptic hinge of some sort, and gum-wrappers
       under the cushions .
        the dog's old
bone, a few strings of gristle still
     glued to one knuckle .
         your favorite block-printed
   silk tie flecked with tiny beige scabs and

                coming unstitched at the point, one
                              rancid maroon sock
                                      and dusty-green
                jockey briefs at the back of the closet under
                        the stiff black shoes
                                   you never wear . old bills,
                     warranties expired, tax receipts,
                pennies in a cracked cup . and late-60s
                              clothes—Nehru shirts,
                                      bell-bottoms, flowers
                and awning stripes . a frowsy wool coat, worsted, good
                        for another season,
                                      expensive wide-wale
                     corduroys too heavy and big
                to wear now too tight come November

                                 —That's not a wardrobe you're packing,
                        that's a first draft: you
                fleshy and white under fluorescent tubes
                              in front of the full-length mirror, notes
                                      scratched on a napkin, illegible
                here where the pen tore through and there
                              where the hand paused in thought, dog
                                 at the edge of the road
                        the first or third or twentieth try at it.
                                 Bring it along, the whole untidy
                     nest of it, or sort
                and toss out. Pack up the broiler pans,
                              scorched and crusty, the cookie sheets
                                      glazed red-brown,
                wrap the old saucers in newspapers, reglue
                        the slats in the ladder-back armchair,
                                 put your records back in their
                     sleeves back in their jackets.
                                 —Do you want this old print from
                        the Dehli museum, the one you meant to get framed?
                Or this rusted eroded scroll from an iron gate?
                              It's not so bad, it's worth doing or
                                 has to be done, worth it
                to carry it all to the new location, what you
                        can carry, what you still want.
                                 Think of unpacking, think about
                        starting again—the cabinet doors
                swing on their hinges, the drawers in the butternut dresser
                              slide smartly closed,
                                      and your better-dressed
                past puts up his feet and smiles, at home
                        with chair rails and ceiling moldings,

> with the high clear
> curtainless windows, and those
> tremulous abstractions,
> parallelograms,
> shimmering on the waxed wood floor .

fall evening
by George Klawitter

If you should find my poems when I am dead,
Remember me, sweet man, remember me
As one who loved you quietly, one lost
In mists of wonder, veiled in simple awe.

Stand naked on your deck, above your head
The pecan trees weaving in the free
Autumn sky, unclouded, awaiting frost,
The sentinels of leaves dropping raw

Reminders at your feet that often we
Would skip our clothes for freedom at the lake,
Enjoying sun and water, changing roles

Of deep and dark responsibility
For open flesh and hair. So turn and take
Into your house my words, tumescent souls.

honor among soldiers
—July 1538; Cuzco, Peru; in the presence of Hernando Pizarro, soldiers, a priest, and the executioner
by Randy Koch

Hernando, my time has come. I've calmed down. Put me where you will and test the rope. I'm past begging and only regret that my trust in you and Gonzalo—out of respect for Francisco—saved you from this fate. The cordillera, too, was cold, deadly, long, but I survived it and returned from the desert to Cuzco. This is all part of the journey.

Take my body and bury me in Our Lady of Mercy. I'll have some peace then. I've seen men die, and I know that even in death they are not still—drawing into themselves, stiffening, and collapsing in the cold, or swelling—stomachs, hands, and legs blistering and bursting like putrid flowers. How can they rest when their bodies are always in motion?

Bury me whole. Don't leave my head on a pike in the sun. Show me that bit of kindness, a last sign of respect for one who has grown as old as I have. You should live so long and come to so abrupt an end. Here I die facing you, who I thought was a brother as your brother was to me. I suppose it's better to die even in the company

of enemies, of friends become enemies than to die alone, where the late thumping of the heart counts away the last moments of life, where my words would be the thin babbling of one gone mad, for what good are words if they fall on no ears? Better they should fall on deaf ears. At least then they have a place to settle until some years later they speak themselves and are finally heard, even if just faintly, like a whisper in the desert or like the wind playing—as in a flute—through the holes of a skull.

I can go on if permitted, but no. Bring the rope—I'll be quiet then—and bring this to an end.

* *Diego de Almagro* (1475-1538), like Francisco Pizarro, was born illegitimately and never learned to read or write. He came to the New World in 1514 and settled in Panama in 1519. He formed a partnership with Pizarro to explore and conquer the country south of Panama along the Pacific Ocean. During the first two expeditions, they learned of the great wealth of the Inca Empire, and in 1529 Holy Roman Emperor Charles V gave Pizarro permission to conquer Peru. By 1533 Almagro and Pizarro completed the conquest of the country, and in 1535 Almagro was named governor of New Toledo, the land south of Pizarro's grant. During 1535-36 he conquered the northern part of what is present-day Chile and then claimed the Incan capital of Cuzco as part of his grant. Pizarro, however, claimed Cuzco as his own, and when Almagro invaded the city, civil war broke out between the followers of Almagro and those of Francisco Pizarro and his brothers Hernando, Gonzalo, and Juan.

Almagro's forces were defeated at the battle of Las Salinas, in which more than 150 Spaniards were killed; he was then captured, tried, and sentenced to death. He begged for his life, but when Hernando Pizarro, who later spent twenty years in a Spanish prison for his actions and died a centenarian, refused to appeal the sentence, Almagro was garrotted in prison and publicly beheaded in Cuzco's square.

impressionists
by Teresa Joy Kramer

Monet's work makes me smile, the bold
brushstrokes—sunflowers, yet not
realistic enough to depress.
They remind me of arrangements

I used to create for the living room
of our cabaña in the village above
the pollution of Mexico City—
enchanted by the mystery of life

with a man who knew everything
I didn't and who loved.
I used to walk to the Quajimalpa mercado,
eat tortillas, fresh, warm,

and select a half-dozen flowers on stems.
My favorites were the wide purple blooms
I'd position in a sweeping arch
on our coffee table for a week,

at least, until wilted petals became
too many to ignore,
even in that poorly lit room.
I ended up leaving that table

and its large, matching sofa, its armchair.
Those carved feet of dark mahogany
were all yours before I came, and before
I left.

secrets
by Bruce Lader

Dora had no need for the *meshugga* language
I was learning, relatives and friends
were landsmen who understood. When I'd ask
about her youth, she'd say, hands trembling
with Parkinson's, "*Zeis kind*, I didn't
go to *shul*; you learn Yiddish."

How in my world of preparing Bar Mitzvah,
mastering Chopin, and playing baseball,
was I going to preserve a dialect
dwindling like memories of the old country
she preferred to forget? Besides,
the stuff she gossiped with my mother
they wanted to keep secret from me.

Frustrated hearing only the mother tongue
when my grandma was present,
I questioned my grandfather and parents,
trying to gather elusive fragments—
like belongings abandoned in Romania—
of the world everyone else wanted to leave,
and they took me to task for being a *nudzh*.

I listened between the notes of joyous
folk singing for clues of the woman
who had shared her small Hester Street
apartment with a homeless immigrant,
brought the child up a second daughter;
I studied photos of her in London at fifteen,
sunning with cousins, footloose with laughing
girlfriends in the Catskills; I watched her

work the sewing machine, arthritic fingers
agile as they crafted miles of thread,
embroidered blouses, aprons, kerchiefs
she would give to friends. I remember
her stoical *tsuris*, love translated
into cooking beyond belief, the freedom
in Zion America she'd say means everything.

watching your sleeping face
riding through the mountains of novy mir
by Mary Ann Larkin

Hurtling
through your grandfather's mountains,
I want to take my hands,
as though I were God
and you some lump of clay,
and gently, firmly
move the high narrow bone
of your nose
to its center.
I want to feel your bone
true under my hand.

I want to make you
who you would have been—
but for wars and bad food—
not the skinny immigrant boy
pummelled by schoolboy fists,
bloody face banging up and down
on a sooty Cleveland playground.

And I want us *not* to be
in this railway carriage
rushing toward our separate worlds,
past the slopes of Novy Mir,
where you never
rode a small white pony
ahead of your friends,
sun polishing your boy-satin skin.

the rain
by Daniel W. K. Lee

What did you think? That Eternity overcame the rain?
Thus defeated, Lover with Beloved conspired to frame the rain.

The preamble concluded and madness, like Eden, bloomed.
For love's abrupt biography, the heart too took aim: the rain.

Of Earth's disgraced empires who waged the same error—
Romans, Mongols, Ottomans tried fatally to claim the rain.

Which clans are pardoned? Who, with grace, remains?
Surely not parties of grief who contrive to blame the rain.

Not bureaucrats of heaven, nor files of mortal prayers;
The oracle whispers: *Even the Divine wavers to tame the rain.*

Press an ear against his pillow and heed the dark refrain:
Only joy that reaps pain can—at once—maim the rain.

He tries to dull the diamond blade, tries to slow the slaughter—
He who tries to halt a holocaust, tries to rename the rain.

Please do not take photographs only to forget my name.
How did I perish in Memory's attic—the flame? the rain?

I finally wrote that poem for you Daniel. How does it begin?
"Death was a mere formality for your bones became the rain."

reporting from fallujah
by Gary Lehmann

I think it was the noise of the hob-nail boots on the stairs at the end of the hall that first woke me. In a place like this an abduction or disappearance is always possible and it pays to make some plans. I jumped from my bed and straightened the covers, throwing two pillows against the wall. I grabbed my bath robe and paddled toward the sliding glass door that led to the open porch. As I passed through the door, I slipped the latch so it would lock behind me as I went out. I just closed it, when I began to hear the pounding of a bludgeon and the shouts of angry men. I crawled under the plastic table and backed myself into the far corner of the tiny porch. Then I reached out for the leg of one chair to further obstruct the view. That was all I could do.

over café
by Raina J. León

Ella tenía 15 años
cuando ella dió a luz a Jesús.
bow your head at the name
of holiness manifest
wonder if you will even have breasts
at the age of the Mother
you are so small
'Buela puts you between the table

and the wall to eat

Mira! Que hermosa ella es.
you see plastic go fleshy
her face changes to Borinquen
goddess of the island and sea
she browns like a beach bikini girl

Mandamos nuestras oraciones a ella.
you bury your eyes in chipped paint
notice the red lines at her eyes
where your cousin has drawn
in the blood tears of miracles
you know will be the only sighting
of crying Mary in North Philly

Ella es la Virgen María.
you nod and drink
el café burns down like doctrines
like penance
you worship the statue early
while the Madonna sings her devil songs
"just like a prayer"

moonrise, hernandez, new mexico 1941
(ansel adams)
by Lyn Lifshin

past adobe, deep behind tumbleweed
someone shuts off a radio, as if news
of war would come over the sage, slither thru
dust and locusts. Under a pale moon
crosses gleam. In streaked light

a young girl unbuttons a hand-me-down
blouse, lets it fall to the linoleum,
thinks of her brother crawling on his belly
in the South Pacific. Her breasts swell, her
hair smells of pinyon and agave.

She hears her father playing banjo on the front porch,
thinks of her mother's leathery skin, lank hair,
swears it won't always be like this: nights with
nothing but the wind in the mesquite,
vows to escape, make it to a place where there is more
than sky and mountains, where women dress in high heels

and smell of roses like in movie magazines

maybe get all the way to
Albuquerque

i am a shoe
for J.B.
by Raymond Luczak

I am a shoe in need of a right-sized foot. I ache
to have him slip inside me, wriggle his toes
comfortably as I walk with him everywhere.
No one would know how much I love him.

I know each crack of the cement ahead of me.
Each story of my past would surely break
my mother's back if she knew what I've done.
The feet in my life would trample her heart.

I am a shoe softened by fuzzy socks
that keep me warm and dry inside on
days that chill and nights that pour.
Each time a toe nudges me, I reawaken.

I am a shoe ready to itch from athlete's
foot. Secrets that shouldn't happen did.
I should be kicked every which way, but no,
the grass forgives me everything I am not.

I am a tired storyteller with legends yet
to fabricate. My yarns snap in half
like worn-out shoelaces. I am way too old.
Contours of my inner sole remain unfilled.

throwaway kid
by Steven Manchester

creeping shadows, silent screams
hidden scars and twisted dreams
bars of steel that block moonbeams—
how did I end up here?

wolves and sheep, a vicious game
concrete walls and tons of blame

neglect, abuse; the stinging shame—
where did my childhood go?

burning hatred, stay in shape
no more victim—
no more rape!
cells or projects, no escape—
when will I heal this pain?

sticks and stones, a bloody knife
words or fists, the constant strife
true survival, not quite life—
but who would even care?

some regret for what I did
twelve-years old and second bid
known to few; a throwaway kid—
why was I ever born?

oasis
by Jeff Mann

There are no poems here,
only coconut fried shrimp
with pineapple dipping sauce,

plumeria fluming
orange and pink,
vivid as flame charring

the fingers of the dead.
On the top deck of the Oasis,
we lie naked all morning

in sun's hibiscus-flare.
Midafternoon, hot tub
bubbles finger our thighs,

rainbows glitter
in our chest hair,
pina colada boys breeze by,

serving weak drinks
we doctor with coconut rum.
Midnight, we kiss beneath

arches of banana leaves
shredded by years of storm,
the warm water steams around us.

Your mouth ranging over me,
I lean back into the light
of waxing moon's

pale grapefruit, tropical stars.
Wind's the only lyric,
rustling dryly in palms.

1962
by Jaime Manrique

I made the kites
myself using
onion paper
the color
of dream
jungles.

With the arrival
of the trade winds
in December
I flew kites at dusk
in Recostadero Park
where Barranquilla's
sweethearts met.

The days
flew by
like kites
in the wind.
At night,
exhausted from kite-flying,
I lay in my bed
neither boy nor man
and night-dreamed
with a kite that flew
all the way to the bloody
moon of the tropics
while below,
on planet earth where
I lived,
all the glaciers melted

all the seas overflowed
and the African continent
went up in flames.

return to the country of my birth
by Jaime Manrique

As I arrive in my old country
the smell of ripe mangoes
welcomes me.
In the fruit trees
sated birds sing:
"It's a good season,
food is abundant,
in many flavors."

At home awaits an e-mail
from my friend Tatiana:
"I am sad—my brother
was killed in the war.
I've returned from the country
of our birth to the cold north."

Later, lured by the smell
of honeysuckle,
I walk in the garden
of the ancestral home.
The air teems with black moths.
Moistened by moon glow
the cannon balls glisten,
hibiscus offer
their lustrous red tongues.

When the moon transits
out to sea, in the high branches
vampire bats feed on
broken-necked nightingales,
and the stars' light reveals
corpses lounging on the grass,
ruby hearts cupped
like split-pomegranates
in their hands.

Back in the house
I answer my friend's e-mail.
"All these dead people
among the plants,
are too much for my first
night back home.
Sorry, but I
did not recognize
your brother among them.
Twenty years away,
I have forgotten
the customs of this place."

in the garden of lope de vega
by C. M. Mayo

A careful, perfect square of a garden. A place for kneeling, weeding by hand. Five trees: parasols of cooling shade. But, surely, never were their ancestors tall enough that, by standing on a kitchen stool, one could not pluck any fruit or nut. What trees were they then, when Lope, with his watering jug in hand, paused in their shade to mop his brow? His garden is four hundred years old (the stone well looks positively Roman) and the grape leaves matted over the pergola might have unfurled themselves, so tender a mint-green, but yesterday.

The west side is bounded by a five storey wall the palest color of a new peach and shocked with sun. It bounces down the rumble of Madrid's noontime traffic and this raking, raking over the dirt— the bits of leaves, feathers, withered rose petals. Such angry, rushed raking— this young woman with sloppy, cherry-fizz red hair in her shapeless, gum-colored trousers. I had said, *Buenos días*, and she went on raking. What do I know of her problems? Or strident, tethered dreams. This cannot be how Lope must have raked.

>He raked: and a face bloomed in his mind.
>He knelt: it dropped the petal of a bawdy pun.
>He heard: the clatter of hooves outside, and birdsong,
>perhaps a child crying.
>The *chiz* of a wasp.
>When, with his jug, he dribbled the silvery well water,
>how it wet this ground like good,
>good words.

passage
by Judith McCombs

A white flag for triumph, flown from the mast height,
the son had promised.
Black if the darkness had covered his eyes.

A life-thread winds like a thread in a maze.
Sun-shapes dazzle,
leap and eddy where cliff meets waves.

Let us not say the palace guard lied:
crows shrouded the mast.
Blame the white webs in the old king's eyes.

Blinded by victory, the son forgot
what hung overhead, and the father
plunged from the cliff. Kingdom and story

passed to the son.

platinum-blond dharma
by Michael Meyerhofer

What else can I do?
Almost enlightened over
two thin volumes
of poetry
from ancient China
and Japan, pondering each word
by the weak lamplight
of a crowded coffee house

when across the room,
she stirs: this young woman
with platinum curls, legs
folding from her sundress like
sleek bronze dolphins,
breasts like Mother Earth
nursing all her stars at once.

Her azure gaze lifts off
a thin art book—perhaps
O'Keeffe's vaginal irises
or Renoir's chubby nudes—

and meets me through
the rising steam of my latté,

long delicate throat tipping
like a soft alighting crane,
rosy fullness of her blushing
just before she
parts her painted lips
and smiles at me.

the games children play
by E. Ethelbert Miller

I.

Their teasing stain my shirt. Their looks throw punches at my head.
I hate school. I dodge and run. Maybe I should kill someone.
I keep a notebook filled with doodles. They say I'm talented and have
a gift. They say I might make a name for myself. I carve my name into
my desk. I make a name for myself. I've got a smile for every newspaper
in the world.

II.

Open the school door.
I've got two bags
and three guns.

III.

Point and shoot. Point and shoot. That's all I do. I'm playing tag with
bullets. I'm it. Rebecca who thought I was crazy looks up from her book.
A few days from now reporters will talk about her courage and how
she managed to survive. After she said she didn't love me I kept missing
her. I miss again.

IV.

Is this paint, chalk or blood on my hands? Maybe it's sweat. I feel like I just
left the gym after making the winning shot.

silent reading
by Larry Moffi

Of everything I never learned or never
learned better, what comes to mind is
reading silently, locking my lips
and the monumental lesson training
both eyes as one muscle inclined
toward a cursor of light, word by word
to mean as far as the narrative
end, when the missionary's daughter,
Martha, tall and pimpled in her moment
of calling jerks the long shade cord
like a magician's assistant and the crude
movie screen disappears.
                        The groan
from the back of the room is the dusty
projector, and here come the questions
in yellow chalk, equations to measure
success: comprehension being the ratio
of rate to retention. What year
did Anaconda Copper begin to mine
Chile? Why did the Otto Frank family
remain in the attic?
                     Years. I've wasted
away dozens of jobs and two increasingly
powerful pair of bifocals. I cannot sing
or dance or remember a joke. I'm still a noisy
reader, a blessing I owe my grandmother,
a Sophie who could not read one word
of English until she had to be loud about
it, in public, as CITIZEN.
                        Evenings
in her kitchen all four daughters, avid
readers of anything, talked her
through the prodigal lives of the fool boy
Dick and his blonde sister Jane until
Sophie's giving mouth found the necessary
shapes despite her twisted accent,
the broken tongue. Mornings she practiced
on me, and I seem to remember the noon
carillon from St. Michael's Cathedral lighting
a time, lips crashing lovely, in waves.

birds of paradise
by Ron Mohring

We stand in the driveway looking first at the garage, its clutter,
so much to be thrown away, then back at the house we have finally
decided to leave. My decision, you remind me, and memory
pins me to the page you're thinking of: how I said With or without
you, I'm going. How ugly the things you keep pressed in your book,
some of them at least, how you flip to those dog-eared pages
just to make yourself feel worse at times. I'd tear them out
if I could, or paste them over with pieces of the man you want
me to be. I grab the rake, you take the broom, and we attack
our chores. The house is up for sale at last, and any day some family
could poke around the garden, open drawers and cabinets—We've got
to hide the toys, you remind me once again—and so this afternoon,
sick of being stuck inside with always more to sort and box,
we spring ourselves: jailbirds on detail, cleaning up the yard.

But that's not true: it's never been a cell, this house of many windows,
home we've tried to make together, physical inheritance I'm ready now
to trade for one last house with you. I offer you the family
you never had, apologize for dragging you away, admit I'll miss
the climate here in Houston. Early March, and roses wave and nod,
oaks dust every surface yellow with their pollen, even the gnarled lantana
sprouts pink-and-orange umbels from what seemed dead wood.
There's no sleeping here, no snow, nothing one could properly term
"winter"—is this why I feel such urgency to get away? With a trowel
you floss the deck boards clean of their trapped leaves, point out
a crab spider's ripped web. The long-necked amaryllis stretches toward
the light. Or is it just the lifted weight of having made the choice?

It's set in motion now: this house will belong to someone else.
If we wait to finish every detail that needs fixing—another coat
of baseboard paint, new edging for the beds, a fresh picket to replace
the piece the neighbor boy broke from the fence—we'll never leave.
We'll leave some work for the new owners. I need quiet pockets,
a place away from helicopters, car alarms, ten-digit dialing.
I need you, and I'm learning to tell you so. You heave the potted
bird-of-paradise onto the deck—it must weigh sixty pounds—and I take out
my pocketknife, trim off the yellowed leaves. This plant was yours
when we met, and I'm insistent that it goes with us, wherever
we end up. Its huge unrolling leaves arch up and out, make me think
of a diver on a board: the upraised arms, the kind of poise that's earned.
But even though we've never seen it bloom—It takes years, you said—
still I must have this plant, not as reminder of where we started out
(though it's that, too), but for the gift it holds concealed, the blossom
coiled somewhere in this green that will unspring one afternoon,

the single purple like a bruise it can't forget completely overwhelmed
by orange, the color of attraction, of opportunity—though you say
you think of love—and isn't that what the two together make?

to erica: transgendered
by Albert J. Montesi

In the stark arena
    Where the mare and stallion
    Fought within you
    What compelled the fusion of your flesh
    Where cells and thought enmeshed?

    The howlings grew:
    "How dare you say to Nature that she failed!
    That you would make it right."

    But now,
    Have you entered a secret garden, Beloved,
    Where things unknown have become known to you
    Where your quest has created an understanding
    That only you and Tiresias shared.
    Of what love is and should be
    And sex a dangling door.

on *día de los muertos* neruda speaks to me
New Orleans, Café Brasil, 2 November 2003
by Kay Murphy

To think, I almost missed the event because every day
is the Day of the Dead. I'm always in black, but this night

everyone is: the orphaned woman in a top hat and dustcoat,
a man in a black wedding gown, a beret pinned with a crucifix.

An altar sparkles with photos; the faint breath
of the posed flickers the candle light that stings their eyes.

Neruda's words are recited in English, Arabic, lispy Spanish.
The Flamenco dancers pound the dance floor to vibrate the dead

into dancing, pound until the small casket I saw in Nepal
needs only a lid and the boy's body, so like my son's.

The drummer's palms pound a wooden drum until the boy's
stiff young body is placed on the pyre, his head to the east.

His mother screams for the third, designated time.
The Lama packs butter onto his soles and his eyelids, into

his ears, his mouth, his anus, so the *alma* when it is time,
can set forth only through the crown aperture. The flesh

burns for hours along with the casket, now splintered
among the juniper branches. But Neruda still has unspoken words.

I do not know the boy nor his mother, unless they are me.
I speak to her in a language only she and I comprehend.

My son, who looks like he has been awakened from the dead,
enjoys this night. Why does it seem that the living suffer

more than the dead, yet the living want only to live?
After the music stops and the dancers bow, Neruda says,

through tongues of fire that lick the living like a dog a wound:
Hurl yourself into your grief like a dove, like snow on the dead.

Not even Neruda on this night knows who are the living, who the dead.

el campo
by Victoria Bosch Murray

My sister kept a tally of my sins, venial
and mortal. She said it would help me get
to heaven were I found like they found that
bebé muerto hidden in the soldiers' pillbox
where we played house in *el campo*, split
top to bottom by the *puta* (a woman
who doesn't like children, she explained).

I was penitent until we found the toy turtle,
abandoned amid the poppies that grew
from the gun-eye slit of the concrete, seven
blocks from the villa where red roses trellised
the stucco. The turtle was taken from us

by a tall girl, like a fig tree wielding a stick
speaking gitano: *Déme la tortuga*.

How much of what I'd seen could I bring
and how much would I have to leave? I ran—
from field to street, one eye shut, into the ravenous
grill of a car; heard its raw squeal, its right eye
bigger than—*¡Madre de Dios!*—the gypsy.
I left my sister, the baby, and the turtle
but took with me the fear of whores.

dusk on the ridge
by Yvette Neisser

The air was dense, filled
with the flames of small fires
and the scent of roasting corn.

It was too late to see the pyramids
or the domes of minarets, now obscured
by the oncoming night—but there below,
in one dry curve of the valley
was a rift between two hills,
their contours blurred
by the jumble of light and dark.

Caught in the sway
of those shifting shadows,
I felt suddenly weightless
as if I were falling into that dip
or suspended on a pendulum
swinging hypnotically
in the space between two solids.

Something opened up
in the unmoving earth,
something unsteadied.

erosion
by Daniel Pantano

When the crisis of the sea announces her anger
the women of the island fasten their clotheslines

hang used panties for the wind to carry their scent
across the triangular land

And as the sea's spontaneous capitulation
adjourns another conquest
the men in the mountains
thank their saint for fertile land

and curse the coastal women for their wretched games

military fantasia
by Richard Peabody

War Movies never get it right

The audience would never stomach the truth.

At Agincourt
the outnumbered English soldiers
were surrounded by bodies of the slain
to a height of 18 deep.

Imagine.

They climbed atop the piles
and continued to bludgeon
and swing their swords and axes
at the demoralized French cavalry.

Antietam.
Bloody Lane.
The first four lines of
Confederate infantry
simply vanished in the grapeshot.

At Verdun
the pigs consumed
the dying and the dead.

Pigs will eat anything
including their young.

Private Ryan is praised for accuracy
yet most soldiers were killed by
the bones of their blown apart buddies
piercing their skin as shrapnel.

Jaw bones, arms, feet,
fragments.

Omaha Beach
bloodier than Hollywood
could ever hope to imagine.

And still we find ways
to send our children to war.

Those who live by the sword
die by the sword.
And that's too good for them.

Those who don't live by the sword
also die by the sword,

too frequently for my liking.

water round the ring of fire
of indonesia
by James Penha

Rain joins two worlds
In the sky on blue water:
Drops of mirror.

The frog hungers—
My blood lives in tadpoles!

Vampires need love
Too despite our hatred
Of the aggressor.

Size doesn't matter—
Life depends on pinpricks.

Monsoon torrents
Halt Jakarta motion:
Contemplation . . .

Floods recede like honey
Sweet season of the sun!

Indonesians summer
With buffalo memories—
Crimson streams.

Windy tarnished evergreen
Overused and overdosed.

When poppies bloom
Even tigers fall asleep:
Ev'ry power wilts.

We are invited
To paradise.

mosquito blizzard
by Kenneth Pobo

Snow again! Icicles build
clear hives from gutters. I

pour tea, remember Wisconsin's
June woods, how I slapped,

cursed mosquitoes, my pleasure
in ferns and mulleins

lost. Today each flake lands,
bites, keeps me inside:

winter's way
of making mosquitoes.

side effects
by Adrian S. Potter

I march proudly, a descendant of slaves and Seminoles
Who has witnessed our culture evolve from different poles
Yet I will never allow tyranny to revoke personal goals
For the sake of my ancestors and their restless souls

I fail to find a state of comfort in this united nation
Knowing that the level of my skin's pigmentation
Directly increases my chances for incarceration
Despite civil rights movements and integration

Forbearers avoided bullwhips by shuckin' and jivin'
Today I dodge police brutality by duckin' and divin'

Run hustles and work jobs, scratching and surviving
Hand money to corporations, while never realizing

That the mainstream media who exploits my soulful style
Fuels the propaganda machine that frames my racial profile
Causing the government to eavesdrop and review my file
Christen me as society's monster before I ever face trial

The side effects of my complexion are not just Negro superstition
If they remain untreated, our country will die from this affliction
A heavy dose of revolution remains the logical prescription
For this disease called prejudice, America's oldest tradition.

la loca de la playa
puerto escondido, mexico
by Emmanuelle Pourroy-Braud

Thighs deep in heaving waves, she stands,
water splashing and whipping against her breasts.
Her soaked ragged shirt sticks to her nipples,
black, icy, raised to dark stormy clouds.
Light blond hair matted with salt and sand,
like an old roving lion's mane,
she interrogates the obscurities of the ocean,
with one question echoed by the swell.

Exiled from *su padre*, wrecked in this port,
five years have passed, but she has found at last
the beach an abode, the water a companion,
the night sky, clear or overcast, a shelter.
Yet, she endures rainy seasons of squalling
winds, standing in dim archways of deserted
downtown alleys like a stilled madonna.

Steeled by the sun, under the bright noon light,
amid natives, foreigners and fishermen,
she sits on the sand, head buried in folded knees,
grounded as rocks on the strand.
With the vacant look of a vagrant as she raises
her head, she lingers within solar flames,
in the blinding bewilderment of the horizon
that loses itself in the blades of the Pacific.

Like a fool with dried, tarred and wrinkled face,
she rises to her feet for necessities and wanders

among vacationers, drenched in the shade of coconuts.
With squinting eyes and hands cupped, she begs,
"un refresco, un sandwich" or "un cigarillo,"
waits and goes. Steered by thirst and hunger,
plodding, watching couples necking,
she reflects the unbearable longing of her spirit.

The mental scars of her past never healed
but harvested only fragments of her vision. At night,
by the monotone growl of specter gray water,
she lies in the leaden cool of the beach,
where no one ventures but white-skinned hunters.
At times when one listens to the ocean roar,
one may hear her screams and wonder.

Tourists rejoice in games of love in the dark.
Across the sandy road from hotel bungalows,
the guttural sound of her voice resounds
under the black, white thundering night
haunted by shrieks of gulls twirling in low sky.
As the prowler's footprints vanish on oozy sand,
the groan in her throat rattles on the shore,
over the surge's wail, blast-blown oceanward.

premonitions
by Maria Proitsaki

I.

I have always known
the day before it would
happen. I collected incidents.
At night I could spell the
tunes of innocent
secrets

Despina would
change her name,
Lena would kill the baby.
And that boy, his spine desiring
another shape, was not to
evade me:

       he wouldn't
stumble and sprawl a wrist—
he headed straight into that

muddy ditch (a-weasel-in-the-
bush-a-fractured-jawbone)

October afternoon
on the cracked edge of the
road, he was bound to meet
my premonitions

II.

When they came,
I would not have them zigzag
the drawer
I wrapped them in lies:
I loved cream cakes and
pitiful Octobers!
Among tampax and
fruit drop pastilles

cheap cologne, cheap earrings
a lump of sugar in the rain
I kept screaming—

lightning in wartime
by Tony Reevy

The storms have hit
every night this week.
A white flash—this is the
first year I've compared
bolts to phosphorus
bombs—and, in five seconds,
the knell of thunder.
I get up, turn off the
computer, a loose-caulked
window rattles—there's
always something—one
of my children wakes.

The night cooling of thick
summer air makes the show,
they say. Not men, not
the turn of A-10's off
a run over Piedmont trees
instead of jungle, desert, the
jagged, broken rocks of Khyber.

the back of my hand
by Kim Roberts

Depending on how they are folded,
        the maps
    resting in the darkened

glove compartments of the cars
        of Europe
    press the city of Vilnius

into the dimpled surface of Poland
        or the flat
    expanse of Russia—

where she could be found in past lives—
        or into the cold blue sweep
    of the Baltic Sea, which wears out

the fabric of mint-green Finland,
        and stripes
    the width of pale pink Sweden

(all the countries the colors
        of candy
    lined up in glass jars):

and this is the way
        Lithuania travels,
    this is the way

Lithuania seeps through my pores
        because
    she loves the dark places,

like the glove compartments
        of the cars
    of Europe,

like the blue veins
        that map
    the back of my hand.

modern malaise
by Peter Roberts

mind,
slow virus,
infects life
—evolution vectored
brain fever.

language,
more virulent still,
infects mind.
we spread the contagion
to chimps & great apes, &
search for the symptoms
in dolphins & whales.

(what
infects
language?)

whitmanesque
by J. E. Robinson

Because yesterday morning I watched your legs, long
and tanned, rise from bare ankles above the floor and
bend under your body as you tied your shoe, Because
last evening I observed you bare your belly when you
lifted your shirt tail to wipe sweat from your brow,
its hair, a nest of feathers and down, matted into
hard, smelly, plastered curls, your belly smooth, pig
white, and hairless, Because I felt your naked hips
against mine all night until early this morning, when
you slipped away to be home in time for breakfast, I
came to the meat department today to see you at work,
to watch you stuff fresh sausages onto their shelves,
to wink at you though the other young men do not let
you wink back and smile that pleasurable smile, the
orgasmic smile you sometimes do, to leave a note on
your windshield—"tonight?"—for you to see on your
way home, and to dream of you, a dream to last all
afternoon, into the evening, too, until I, newly
bathed, hear you coming through the door, removing
your coat and cap, walking up behind me...

buddha breathes
by Joseph Ross

Buddha
breathes in

and every cell
organ and drop of blood
spins and shivers
into ecstasy

Buddha
breathes out

and every bone
stone and waiting tear
settles back
into
silky sleep

numbers
by Marianne Ehrlich Ross

I have died eight times:

Once in my mother's womb

Once, age four, in Vienna on *Kristallnacht*

Once on the German/Dutch border
The day World War Two began

Once, in the London Blitz –
A piece of shrapnel in my featherbed

Once on the operating table
From a ruptured appendix

Once when my sister jumped
From a nineteenth story window.

When my car was totaled
Twice,
By a runaway trailer,
And a rear-end hit.

I'll use my ninth life to stop
America's killing of millions
To begin World War Three
To be Number One

he was a poet and when he died
by Mark Saba

He was a poet and when he died
they buried him in a tree.
They cut a hole three feet wide to dig out pulp
and shoved his body way on down, arms up,
head facing north. Then they filled
the rest with dirt—dirt inside a tree.
The tree grew and it grew and grew
until the hole closed up. Branches turned up
to the sky; leaves came and went
as leaves do. It was a large tree,
very strong: some say it was walnut.
Along came a furniture company and cut
it down. First an ax hit, then it fell
then they took it to shave off bark.
The bark was gone; it looked like
a telephone pole. Then saws ripped it
into boards: perfect two-by-eights;
perfect, glistening, and inlaid with specks
of bone. And some hair.
And guess what? The wood is now in your
home. Tables, drawers, guitars—
Have you ever wondered what it would be like
to be a poet?

puzzles
by Jhoanna Salazar

Six thousand miles away from him,
I tell my father over the phone
that I quit teaching,
that I walked right out

of the classroom without knowing
what I was going to do next.
I hear him sigh, the disappointment
in his breath reaching me

as loud as if he were right
next to me. I picture him
sitting in the yellow
wall-papered kitchen

a crossword before him,
almost done,
a red pen in his hand,
and here I am

calling and spoiling
his answer to 99-down,
which was right at the edge
of his thoughts, but now gone.

What now? he asks,
and all I can give him
is the silence I've been living in,
my days full of not knowing

where I was going. I wanted to stop
discussing it, and, instead, I wanted him
to tell me a clue, and how many letters,
and the intersecting answers

he'd already gotten, and then
we could both think of the possibilities,
see if they fit, one of us eventually
finding the right words.

che bel rimedio*
by V. Jane Scheeloch
> "I can suck melancholy out of a
> song, as a weasel sucks eggs." – William Shakespeare

Suck all the melancholy from the song.
Open your lips just enough to take in
all the pain of the blues, torch songs,
operas about consumptive beauties.
Let the notes hold your tears
like giant black buckets
swinging from high, thin wires.
Gulp the bitter memories,
the broken dreams, the dried up hopes.
Swallow each measure of sadness.
Do not let one sixteenth note of solace spill out

to alleviate the melody
of your own private aria.

* What fine medicine

moskva
by Keith Scotcher

we flew to moscow
to see sestra vikka
in the land of dachas and matryochkas
now coming up modern
ten and twelve lane highways
thundering through city central
hurtling onwards
car crazy capital
where young ruskie dudes crave hot motors
but trusty ladas and volgas still rule the prospekt

a slow train down to stavropol
to see mama shura
reading *catcher in the rye*
along the way
sad visit to the cemetery
sharing bread with the beloved dead
a mother and grandmother
and old vasily who fought the nazis

the long distance bus back to moskva
twenty four hours on a hard road
one and a half thousand k's
with a hundred million sunflowers watching us all the way
and through a hard night
a busload of contortionists try to get some shuteye
all just hoping the driver ain't joinin 'em
the rising sun reflecting off silver birch guardians
and still three hundred k's to go
then the mighty metropolis looms
a bourgeois island in the rural vastness
all rushing   all yelling   all buying   all selling
all   —   forgetting
all   —   joining   —   the age old rat race
whose winner is always the biggest rat

but russia has its own determined pace
its ancient soul indefatigable
old babushkas still grow fruit and sell them by the road
having seen it all
and they know
the blood red fountains of poklonnaya gora
where promenadeers stroll — eat ice cream — and skate
ain't there to advertise coca cola

january
by Gregg Shapiro

Over time, winter in Chicago loses its Arctic edge,
the principle of frigid surprise. Predicted snow
blanketing remaining holiday frills, cars parked
haphazardly along the curb, shingles, pavement,
drain pipes and pedestrians equally. The snowflakes,

liberal and without prejudice, as diverse as the residents
in this sunlight deprived, weatherbeaten neighborhood.
A few weeks into the official winter season, closure
and rebirth, linked permanently together. By the sixth
day of the new year, it's already taking its toll, famous

strangers' names clogging the obituaries. Amidst
the flurry of tardy gift exchanging and tree dismantling,
there is passing mention of appointment book refills
and resolutions. An ex-lover calls with belated holiday
wishes and to tell me that he's found a new boyfriend.

I know I should tell him how happy I am for him,
but all I feel is dizzy, divested of aura and speech.
Is it a sudden change in the air pressure or fear
of being replaced, abandoned, forgotten? Nattily
dressed television weather-forecasters notorious

for their displays of smug boredom, bordering on
amusement, and wizardry with blue screens, issue
warnings in pinched "I told you so" tones. There is
a proper way to shovel heavy, just-fallen snow, to apply
the brakes when a car starts to skid, to cure depression

brought on by the grey veil of winter. At the end
of a day-long storm, there are shimmering street lamps
and headlights, shy fingers of lightning scratching
the sky, and luminescent snow cover. White,
and its variations, corrupted by tire tracks and

exhaust, footprints and animal urine. The blue glow of late afternoon, lingering and insistent, the color of hope. The guarantee of the thaw, the season of longer days and abundant light just beyond the horizon, out of the steadily declining temperatures' greedy reach.

naming
by Marian Kaplun Shapiro

Apple! He tastes the syllables
again, hearing *red, green,*
smelling *sweet with sweet white juice.*
Wordless, his one-year-old fingers
punctuate the air, towards
the refrigerator. *Hah!*
(*There! In there!*)

Wanderers in the Museum of
Antiquities we find ourselves attended
by the ancient Buddhas of Tibet,
by way of China. Gazing down they watch
kindly over us, the unenlightened,
We are tutored by the bodhisattvas,
humble heroes whose names we can't pronounce.
Gladly they waited here on earth, postponing
Nirvana for the sake of those who needed
them. For us. Patience beyond patience.
Blessing beyond blessing. Names beyond names.

In the beginning was the Word

        And the Word,

infinite,   unspoken   unspeakable
    rises,

        rises,
            a transparent
helium
        balloon
            a
                coda of
    ethereal
        echoes

just   out of reach
                    disappearing

    like fog   at sunrise.

            Truth?
or mirage?

            Who are you

God, Jehovah, Supreme Being, Almighty, Everlasting, Eternal, King of Kings, Creator, Yahveh, Adonai, Allah, Buddha, the Atman, Brahma, Goddess. The Spirit. The Light. The Nameless One.

            I am that I am,

        wearing a necklace of old Greek
        coins, silver full moons
        against a dark blouse sky. My newest
        grandson, five months into life,
        leans into his future, fingers
        already expert at the grab. *Ah
        GAH!* he shouts. *(I want it!)*

you don't believe that dromedaries keep moonlight in their humps?
after pablo neruda
by Lucille Gang Shulklapper

I thought you stored my fatty
heart in your hump, reserved its

bloodied vessels to insulate your
heat. I thought you kept white

orchids whispering thirst,
a hummingbird flinging itself

against your flesh, the crush of shells
when the waves ebbed. Perhaps you

    were

bred to race in the desert despite your
rocking, shuffling gait, or a wandering Arab

in search of moonlight. Look for me on
one black night. I want to be your moon.

harmless
by Myra Sklarew

                I want to lie down
on the earth like my cat, to roll
over on my back and let the sun walk
across my face.
             Magdalena Abakanowicz
says art is harmless. "Stalin was a poet.
Hitler was a painter." Says, "Art is the space
between wisdom
             and madness...it opens
our brains to imagining." In this poem
I ask the anxiety of early morning
to stand aside
             like a good soldier who
draws back his bayonet and allows me
to pass by. In this poem I ask that the transport
of frozen children
             be transformed, that
in the morning when they come to unlock
the ice-covered door, from each golden
chrysalis
             a living child will emerge.
That the artist, between dreaming
and reality, opens our eyes and places
before us
             twenty girls, intact.

for contemporary historians
by J.D. Smith

Herodotus' wide net
could not encompass the present data.
Nor could the focus of Suetonius
locate the most relevant thread.

The age knows itself as an age,
its monologue rolling
across time zones:

your magnum opus might therefore
provide an hour of content
until another magnum opus is called upon
to fill another hour.

Consider the amoeba
that has no fixed form
or constant center,
but with shifting shape
flows through fluid and time.

A culture moves this way.
From within, one can hardly discern
the recent trail, the straightest path,
only sketch the nearest edge, and hope
that it connects adjacent sketches—
that they exist—
and that Caesar or subject might examine them
in passing.

on ice
by Reet Sool

And the snow falls now
on your traces
(and maybe mine)
on the red roof of the opposite house
and the flags
(hanging like rags)
and the monument of the peace treaty
(a peace treaty, really)
one of many
preceded by a war
(one of many)
any
in which young men were torn
into shreds
as were young pines
firs and spruces
this placating snow
on the back of the man that goes
to buy his daily bread

(think of the dead)
on the crosses
and helpless benches
the iron fences
the angels lost in the storm
(the ships lost at sea)
on you
on me—

                all I have of her now
                    is a blue line
                        on ice.

help
by Laurel Speer

Wait a minute.
I may be an accused mercenary in this godforsaken Zimbabwe jail,
but I'm a civilized human being. I have some rights,
and I deserve consideration.
Now the authorities have ordered around-the-clock leg irons
because someone reported plans for a jail break.
I have sores where the irons chafe.
I need to bathe, exercise, walk.
What about personal hygiene?
I'm a human being here, not a mercenary.
I was on my way to Congo to give mine security,
but they got me tied up with some plot in Equatorial Guinea.
Come on. Do I look like the kind of guy
who'd commit himself to mayhem and certain death
for the pittance they offer desperate and pathetic mercenaries?
This is injustice and causes skin infection.
It's demeaning.
Help.

voyage
by Judith Strasser

      Life begins when the children
      leave home and the dog dies.

There is no dog. But the cat
sleeps with me now, burrowing
under the comforter to curl
in the curve of my belly

and thighs. Unless evening
beckons, and he, too, leaves,
nosing the screen door open
to prowl all night outside.

A poet said this is rehearsal
for death: all these departures,
the one-time friends whose lives
have taken a different turn;
the children, so distant
their rooms have given up clutter
and scent; the husband who couldn't
suffer emotion; the mother-in-law
a few months gone, herself a stand-in
for a mother who died long ago.

Death could not be so hard.
It's you that goes, and either
it's heavenly—you meet the mother
again, and dear departed pets—
or it's eternal nothingness
but you have no way to care.
This is life: you headed
into the void, hurtling
through darkness, passing
stars sharp streaks of light.

saxophone
by Dan Stryk

First to worship
           Sun & Moon,
leg weavings
           of the ant or fly
over the outdoor table's
      sheen,
           the raucous
jay's blue whirr
at the eye's edge
           overhead,
      its muted notes
of wingtip grey,
as well —
           and *then*
           the grunting sting
           of SAXOPHONE,

```
    purr of brass scales
                    or sudden
                brazen screech
                of wind
                        as fingers
        of the mind
                run over pulsing
                keys that pierce
                twin hearts
of bass & drum,
life's thumping prayer.
```

november and november and november
by John Sweet

later
with the shadow of each house
crawling up the one
beside it
with this man lumping blindly
from the bridge into the river

with the smokestacks pressed hard
against the frozen blue sky
and this idea that what lies beyond the hills
is the rest of the world

the things i've lost
possibly

my father's small death

my grandfather's suicide

and i remember a letter from a stranger
telling me that none of this shit
i was writing could be called poetry
and i remember the poem
i sent to him

i remember the taste of the girl
who told me
she didn't believe in love

the cigarette burns on
her soft white stomach

the windows veined with frost
all of these
cold shadowed rooms
we would never call home

why i love florence
by Hilary Tham

Water is not my element. Lake grass conjures
                tentacles and monster mouths.

Fire is not my element though I love
                to watch its dance, scarves of flame
singing arias in a language
                I do not know.

Air is not my element though flying
           does not bother me. Like stone, I do not fear
                falling back to earth.

Earth is my element. Some *when*
I must have been stone—child of Earth's
                ribs— stone pushing up
a mountain, stone holding up a home,
cobblestone laughing, tickled by sandaled feet.
Once, I was stone arm
           falling from a statue
                down to the safe, soft
                        bottom of a brown river, the wind
scrubbing the lines of my name
                from the water's skin.

what moves us
after Kathleen Raines
by Hilary Tham

The brain drives the body.
Within the brain rests a cauliflower,
cauliflower that images an oak.
An oak, occupying space, spreads
elongated fingers into the blue of sky,
roots its toes into dark interstices of earth
mirroring its branches,
branches that bear acorns green

as early lemons.
Within the lemons—captured sunlight;
within a courtyard of stone walls.
Within the walls, a well
holding darkness
and water.
Within the water, memory
of church bells and sky;
within the memory of sky, the whiteness
of clouds that glide high above
the bodies of humankind
toiling in the fields of sun-warmed grain,
silvery olives and ripening grapes—
San Giovese —sangre di Giove
the blood of Jove grapes.
Within the blood, the throbbing
need for love and light
rising up through the branching veins
to the brain.
Within the brain, the compressed soul—
soul folded over and under and into itself
taking in stone walls, well, water,
trees: lemon, oak, olive.
Soul unfolds and stretches
light as wind and moves
silently across the world.

bicoastal:
the sell date on my life has expired
by Gloria Vando

I dream I'm in New York City,
wake up in California, walk
into the wall. I turn right to
go to the bathroom, walk into
a closet. I'm out of toilet
paper, even though I bought 12
rolls at Safeway 5 days ago.
I turn on the cold water, scald
myself. It's five a.m. I'm out
of milk, the eggs are three months old.
Vital files have vanished from my
computer. I hear it dial unfamiliar
staccato notes. No DSL.
The signed Karl Shapiro on my

bedstead is by Martín Espada.
The clothes in my closet are two
sizes too small, my favorite
jacket is gone. Where are my shoes?
I'm afraid to drive the car—it's
a hybrid. I drive north, wind up
in Baja with strangers, who look
familiar. Back home, my husband
storms into the living room. "Can't
find my watch, can't find my wallet."
A mere trifle. I can't find myself!

positive images
by Shelley Ann Wake

The psychology professor
read from a textbook:
"You grade yourself
via comparison with others.
If your view of yourself is low
Compared to others,
your self esteem is low."

So I sat in the classroom
with 100 ordinary people
and conducted
my comparisons.

I looked around the room
at the average, the ordinary,
even the reasonable.
I knew nothing of them.

I thought of the others I see so often,
the successful, the beautiful,
the exceptional.
I know them.

Tom Cruise, Thomas Edison,
Michael Jackson, Michael Jordan,
Jennifer Aniston, Jennifer Lopez,
Bill Clinton and Bill Gates.

The professor said something else
about low self esteem,

but I wasn't listening.
I was too depressed.

finally in autumn
by Davi Walders

Finally in the Morvan
autumn rain streams
from pregnant clouds.
Parched hills exhale
their unhappiness,
suckling at heaven's breast.
The long grey dying surrrenders,
swelling with green life.

reunion
by Amelia Walker

Some of us got old
and some of us got older, faster
some of us are already dead.
And some of us are married
and some divorced
and some with kids
and some still living
with mum and / or dad
or both, or neither.
Some, sleep in a different bed
every Saturday and some
haven't got a bed at all.
Some have good jobs
and some give head jobs
some don't want to leave
university, and some
never went there in the first place.
Some went mad
and some got even
some, have travelled the world
some sit on the couch
watching 'Getaway'.
Some of the pretty girls got ugly
and the ugly girls got pretty.
The cool boys became public servants
with bald spots. The uncool boys

became high paid professionals
with bald spots.
Some play the pokies
some trade stock
some take Zoloft
and some take smack.
Some go to church, some
to the gym, some read Sartre
some Harry Potter, some
just wish they could walk again.
Some have cancer, and some
still smoke. Some failed suicide
and some got it right
or wrong, or whatever. Some
jumped from planes
and wondered at the view.
Some attempted life.

lying in bed
by Jeff Walt

I never imagined us with grey hair, or these bellies
we can't get rid of no matter how many StairMasters
we climb. The wrinkles around our eyes

like miniature highways remind us where we've been,
where we're headed. I rub the calluses on your palm.
A day of lifting rocks from the new garden. Delight

as if discovering your body for the first time—flesh
flabby as my grandmother's bread dough under your arms,
capillaries blossoming on your face; blades of hair

sprout out your ears. There is no part of your body
my tongue hasn't met, know it as well as my own.
I've learned to love my small sliver of this unkempt bed,

your snoring, the comfort of the sagging mattress, moaning
box springs and loose headboard that bangs the wall
when we toss and turn. I shut off the light, pull the bundle

of rumpled covers over us like the warm years we've lain together.
My pulse against your back reminds me how alive I am.
Our exquisite middle-aged bodies spooned, flawed, and used.

miss kitty's blues
by Jeff Walt

I sit here at the kitchen table playin' cards with myself.
Sit here half the night talkin' to myself.
Maybe whiskey's all that's kept me in good health.

God help me 'cause I know I'm a drunk.
God help me 'cause I want to get drunk.
I miss singin' jukebox songs with my good friend Skunk.

Men tell me I'm fine, but I ain't believin' that shit.
Tell me I'm fine and I still feel like shit.
Say they want me in their kitchen, but I'll never get hitched.

I want Mitch's bar and the jukebox pulsing red & blue light.
I want my usual stool and a stranger offering me a light.
I need Jack Daniels and lots of *Walkin' After Midnight*.

I been like a dog tied inches from the bone of pleasure.
I been good for weeks—now I need to dig up some pleasure!
I want a wild night that will howl forever.

I might go downtown and shop for a little noise.
I might go for just an hour to guzzle down a little noise.
I could have just one—maybe buy a round for the boys.

If I go, I'll promise to be back by midnight.
God, I promise I'll be back by midnight.
I need a little somethin' to make me feel right.

I grab a ten, my cigs, dart for the door.
I grab my jacket and keys and run out the door.
Two shots later I'm spinning with a trucker on the dance floor.

to my ex-lover making a commitment
   for jason, burlington, vermont 9/28/01
by Jeff Walt

It is not the Justice of the Peace I see in front of me
as the Wedding March starts, or the guests
dressed in tuxedos, leather and drag, but that tiny
apartment on Pearl Street: the bed shoved
up against the stove with only two burners, one element
broken; a shower the size of a telephone booth; the rusted

refrigerator groaning; noise from the street jangling
through the two rooms. Both of us making minimum
wage in jobs we hated. I see the night we burned
incense and, vowing never to give up, built our dream
house out of magazine clippings—a collage to remind us
of where we were going, like the self-help book suggested.
Nights of too much wine and fighting: whose turn
to take out the trash, Where were you? and Why
did you look at him that way? Fists, broken glass, blood,
black & blue years of trying. Friends now, forgiveness
a lost charm found. Love, as I walk you down the aisle,
I don't want to let go. These minutes are like the end
of a difficult fairy tale where two have found light at the edge
of the woods after a dangerous journey together and must
say goodbye—I pause for a silent moment to hold you
and then press your hand firmly in his; I give you away

coming home
for todd and angie
by Charlotte Warren

Soon our arms are around each other, and stay there.
It's midnight. Like a myna bird,
dazed after twenty-one hours of plane rides,
I chatter while our son drives,
the city lit and unwinding around us.

Those young trees just beyond the streetlight
remind me of how he and his wife
stood out in the crowd,
moving easily forward in their welcome
even though the stain of the world
had already washed their eyes clear.

Now it's their driveway.
But before he sets the handbrake
I'm opening doors to the sweet
night air, the blossoming cherry and plum
floating out of the dark
the way their faces floated into view at the airport.

On the other side of the world
a cold rain turns
to snow in the mountains.
Here, too, it rains,
but to coax a different season,

one where even the stars
break the dark with promise.

passing as a mulatto
by Allison Whittenberg

Four sisters were playing, laughing
The lightest one bragged,
'If we were back in the day,
I would be house.'
Then pointed. 'And you
would be house.'
Then pointed again. 'But yall two
would be field.'

>This girl judged like an overseer
>She felt she could since
>She was practically
>a white person,
>except for the fact
>she had two black parents

(Not all black is black
Not all black comes from cotton,
The ghetto, primitive jungles)

>She spent that winter,
>passing as a mulatto,
>showing her near white hands,
>keeping her nappy hair
>under a scarf

dora circa the war years
by Allison Whittenberg

For remembrance week, the picture of Dora's girlish dark-haired
freshness and a taut, three-paragraph bio were posted

For that week, in the courtyard, co-eds passed her, too wrapped in
their own stressors and crosses-to-bear to notice

Hiding, maneuvering,
creating a bottomless sense of chaos,
she had spent her wonder years as a partisan

making, makeshift weapons out of lost parts,
sleeping in forests,
using her machine gun as a pillow

Evading, plotting,
breathing almost to the date of liberation
she had escaped ghettos,
trains rides, liquidations
until too many Germans surrounded,
demanding the villagers produce a Jew
disarmed, momentary solidarity melted to basic instinct
someone pointed out Dora

They bound her hands
tied a rock to her neck
threw her in the river
then shot her twice

An empty, gray ending to a would-have-been full, green life
under other circumstances...

nights before christmas
by Fred A. Wilcox

Walking home from a party
Where I drank hot mulled cider and rum
The lights are lovely snow and a friend
Sings hello tis the season tis
I see a monk in the window
Watch him remove his robe
And step into a steaming bath.
Ten thousand miles away
A Chinese soldier penetrates
A young Tibetan nun
The monk screams, sinks
Into incense sprinkled water
Eyes open to the next incarnation
And when they drain the tub
He is smiling like
An innocent young girl.

asking directions
by Jill Williams

When they don't know. That's when it drives me nuts.
And still they mutter, "Six blocks past the light."
To lie like that to strangers takes some guts.
But lie, they do, until I'm out of sight.

And still they mutter, "Six blocks past the light."
They'll mention names of streets that don't exist.
And lie, they do, until I'm out of sight.
It's some compulsive need they can't resist.

They'll mention names of streets that don't exist.
To say 'I just don't know' would seem too weak.
It's some compulsive need they can't resist.
And I am left so pissed I cannot speak...

To say "I just don't know" would seem too weak.
Most men—for sure—will never let it pass.
So I am left too pissed to even speak,
Directionless without a drop of gas.

Most men—for sure—will never let it pass.
To lie like that to strangers takes some guts.
Like mouthing lewd remarks and pinching ass.
When they don't know. That's when it drives me nuts.

pure jazz
by A. D. Winans

intense convoluted horn solo
old Diz filling the room
with his raging truth
Miles Davis and his lyric
savagery cutting to the bone
slicing its way to the center
force of gravity
lubricating the gears
of my mind
whose pigments of indigo
disguised as blue float
through the blue haze air
echoing latitudes of motionless
motion

an arab dreamer and i dream the same dream
by Ernie Wormwood

We dreamed the war was over
We dreamed the moon mooning through our windows at midnight
We dreamed flowers growing from our pens
We dreamed Mary Poppins bringing us a spoonful of sugar laced with Rumi
We dreamed the Baghdad Museum had not been bombed
We dreamed video cameras in prisons everywhere for the Safe Prison Channel
We dreamed all despots in the same work release program
      where they must search for
           weapons of mass destruction for as long as they all shall live
We dreamed our descendants wearing the peace of the world they live in
We dreamed of the poets
We dreamed the war was over
We dreamed all war was over.

loki
by Gerard Wozek

I asked Loki for a sign
at the crossroads. He said,
Enter darkness. I asked Loki
for the well in the desert.
He said, *Become seed
on the barren plain, stem
of the chokeweed, last
breath of the dandelion.
Bloom anyway.* I asked Loki
for the map to knowingness
He said, *Honor your questions.*
I asked Loki for a spirit
companion. He said,
*Find the trailhead to the path
of the androgyne within.*
I asked Loki, if I could be
gooseflesh, tingle, blood rush.
He said, *Be hungry.*
I asked Loki for reprieve.
He said, *Trust in the world
spinning unnoticed in you.*
I asked Loki for a wing
or a shadowy cape

so that I could be night.
He said, *There are no escapes.*
I asked Loki if I could be
fire, in order to fleck off sparks,
give off heat, blaze into the dark,
like some prophesy or godhead.
He said, *Beware.*

the country of us
by H. E. Wright

edges shoot deep into the soil, planting the foundations into solid
limits—where, previously, there had been only
intricately dotted border tracings, whose chief
function was to make a simple map of us

read more colorfully. to distinguish me from you, us from them. from
outside or in the boundaries, the lines are now
somehow fleshy, crude, cold as granite—not
ethereal or neat suggestions,
not intellectually chosen abstractions
for holding together the symbolic order of places and their things.
each fenced field is full of a pensive and
loud ghost, trampling the moors, a ghost who probably—

in the topography of all these years—

did not matter all that much, but who refuses, now, to ever go away.

language of the earth
by Katharina Yakovina

My language is my tree.
My language is my bird.
My language is my sea.
My language is my sky.

I write my messages to people.

Their language is war.
Their language is indifference.
Their language is envy.

If they lose the language of love
Then I will stop to write them.

French Poems

la musique
par Robert L. Giron

Violons
Boléro danse d'amour
Marseillaise libre nuit et jour

dans un sac en osier
par Colette Michael

Je longe
la grève sablonneuse
face à l'immensité
tentée
de laisser là
dans un sac en osier
souliers et soucis
de ce monde dégénéré
d'entrer
droit devant moi
comme dans un sanctuaire
avec respect
dans cette mer huilée
de paix
d'éplucher
comme un manteau
trop lourd à porter
les amours
qui brûlent
feu de pailles
les lâchetés
mensongères
et de laisser là
dans ce menhir
à ma taille
les rancunes
et les torts
mais partir
à l'abandon
vêtue des joies
en filigrane
bronzée par
les souvenirs
les mains ouvertes
vers l'oblivion

l'autre face de l'empire
par Mutombo Nkulu-N'Sengha

Ida, ma soeur
Ne pose pas la question
Cette question de chez-nous
Où travaille-t-il ?
Combien gagne-t-il ?
Où est-elle ?
Où va-t-elle ?
Ici on ne pose pas de question
Ces questions du village

Ida, ma soeur
Tais-toi, s'il te plaît
Ici c'est la ville
Ne discute pas ma soeur
Tes villageois vertueux
sont en guenilles
et vivent de chenilles
Ici c'est l'abondance
de mondes et d'immondices
dans l'empire des vampires
C'est le prix de la liberté
Tais-toi, ma soeur

Ida, ma soeur
Ne pose pas de question
Ne cherche pas à comprendre
Tes ministres lavent les cadavres
Tes princesses balaient les ruelles
Tes princes dorment à la gare-Termini
Sur des lits de poussière
Lisière de la liberté !
Récompense du progrès!
Ici on ne pose pas de question
Ces questions du village

Ida, ma soeur
Ne pose pas de question
Tes princes sont chefs le jour
La nuit ils deviennent esclaves
Tes ministres lavent les assiettes
Ils vendent les biscuits dans les rues
Adieu dignité africaine
Maxime des chercheurs d'or
Tout le monde est content

Ici tout se vend
Ici tout s'achète
Dieu et le Diable
La foi et la loi
le pouvoir et le valoir
C'est le conte des fées
Dans un monde des fées
Dans un monde du feu...
Ma soeur ne pose pas de question
Ici on n'écoute pas ces questions
des primitifs du village.

L'exil est une bombe
L'exil est une tombe
Tout exil est servitude
Tout exil est platitude
On est Prince chez-soi
On est prince sous son toît
On est prince au village
Là où brille les astres des ancêtres
Ma soeur c'est là qu'on pose des questions
de dignité et de liberté
de fraternité et de fierté
Ici on ne pose pas de question
Ici on n'écoute pas
Ces questions du village.

l'astronome
par Emmanuelle Pourroy-Braud

L'astronome vaillant, comme le capitaine
Tenant habilement la barre à gouverner,
La Polaire et Vénus l'aidant à se guider,
A l'art de naviguer sur l'onde souveraine.

Par une soirée d'hiver glaciale et hautaine,
L'amateur qui, craintif, frileux, ne peut sonder
Le secret d'une nova variable et lointaine,
Sollicite Uranie et rentre se chauffer.

Mais quand une telle nuit sans lune se dénude,
L'initié se remet promptement à l'étude,
Malgré et en vertu du temps qui se poursuit.

Alors ses yeux fervents et curieux se dessillent
Sur la voûte houleuse de l'espace infini,
Car les céphéides dans l'empyrée brasillent.

errant
île amantani, lac titicaca
par Emmanuelle Pourroy-Braud

Quand les jours imposaient l'amitié
Quand les rivières sifflaient liberté
Quand la Croix du Sud apparut
      plus belle que la Croix du Nord

Je courrais, transportée, légère.
Au sommet de Pachatata, mes ailes,
aussi larges que celles du condor, se déployaient.

Mais quand, un soir, jeune présomptueuse,
je rompis le contrat de confiance et d'humanité
établi avec mon hôte, mes ailes se brisèrent.

Sur Pachatata, je restais suspendue
à ma conscience égarée, au-dessus d'un lit
de fleurs sans fragrance, sous un soleil radieux.

panégyrique pour l'emmerdeur
—poème dédié à *steak hâché*—
par G. Tod Slone

Il parle quand il faut pas parler.
Il opine quand il faut pas opiner.
Il critique quand il faut pas critiquer.
Ça déprime, ça fulmine, ça sourit ni aux cons ni aux chafouines !

Il touche aux icônes qu'il faut pas y toucher.
Il questionne les règlements qu'il faut pas questionner.
Il met au défi les chefs qu'il faut pas mettre au défi.
Ça secoue, ça éclate, ça rend pas hommages aux ploutocrates !

Il n'applaudit pas quand il faut applaudir.
Il part quand il faut pas partir.
Il boit beaucoup quand il faut pas boire du tout.
Ça brasse, ça culmine, ça fait jamais bonne mine !

Il gueule quand il faut pas gueuler.
Il écrit quand il faut pas écrire.
Il réfléchit quand il faut pas réfléchir.
Ça rouspète, ça proclame, ça s'en fout des vedettes quidams !

Lui, tu sais, n'est peut-être qu'un simple poète maudit !

sous appellation contrôlée... dite liberté
la liberté n'est pas une marque de yaourt.
—Pierre Falardeau, cinéaste et nationaliste québécois
par G. Tod Slone

Que c'est désolant le paysage courant,
si calcaire, si clonique, si cliquaire !

La liberté de parole, oui, mais
coupez-la bien quand ça risque
de vous exposer !
La liberté d'expression, oui, mais
étouffez-la bien quand ça menace
de s'exprimer contre vous !
La liberté de se faire publier, oui, mais
sous des règles qui serrent le cou
la liberté !
La liberté de l'inanité, oui et
répandez-la bien
car ça ne suscite jamais
de la liberté !
La liberté, enfin, oui, mais
toujours dans des espaces prédéterminés
et sous des thèmes préapprouvés !

Oui, le paysage n'est pas tellement encouragent
et oui la liberté n'est pas une marque de yaourt, mais
elle n'est pas non plus une revue qui s'appelle *Liberté* [*] !

---

[*] *La Revue Liberté*, Montréal (www.revueliberte.ca).

N.B. : Deux ans après la rédaction de ce poème, Robert Yergeau a publié *Art, argent, arrangement*, un tome de plus de 700 pages qui examine le rapport entre l'argent d'État et l'artiste au Québec. Pour la revue *Liberté*, il a noté que ses dirigeants affirmaient ouvertement que cet argent entravait la «véritable liberté d'expression». «Mais à partir du moment où ils recevront régulièrement des subventions et qu'ils s'imposeront de plus en plus dans le champ culturel, ils seront bien obligés de changer de discours;

dès lors, le retournement sera complet : loin de brimer la liberté, le mécénat d'État la favoriserait. Opportunisme idéologique? Réalisme tactique?»

enfin en automne
par Davi Walders

Enfin dans le Morvan
vient la pluie coulante
des nues enceintes, étaines.
Les collines ternies exhalent
leur malheur morne, avalent
des cieux ce lait du tétin.
La vie verte est reprise
de la longue mort grise.

Spanish Poems

al poeta que sobreviva
por Luis Alberto Ambroggio

Edad de Oro.
Dicen que de los miles de poetas
apenas tres sobrevieron
en la memoria de los siglos;
y acaso sobreviva sólo uno
de los muchos poetas de nuestro calendario.
Irrescatable el silencio de las siembras
los felices versos.
Deshechados los caprichos de belleza.
Ni siquiera el reciclaje salvará alguna rima.
Quizá se conserve en anónimo un epígrafe
y el polvo que cubra los tormentos.
El río, sí, perdurará en su corriente indescifrable
Y el cóndor se eternizará en su vuelo.
El amor también repetirá sus aventuras.
La muerte seguirá el curso de los cielos.
De los poetas, sólo uno sabrá decirlo
Para las ilusiones de los tiempos que devengan.

¡Cuántas palabras de sobra,
Páginas, minutos, árboles cortados al vicio!

Extinción irreversible.
Entre la multitud, tan sólo un grito
(pedestal único, canonizado).
¡Asombrosa siempre la economía del olvido!

Un grano mínimo de arena
en el eterno murmullo del océano.

Un solo grito.

inocencia
por José Ben-Kotel

Extendió alegre
La mano con la imagen
Que la complace

La tomó y miró
Atento conocía la historia
Risa inmaculada

Observó el azul
Era un océano girando
En el fotograma

Mira le dijo
A su alumna cómplices
Riendo íntimos

Parece un mar
Una constelación un navío
Una galaxia

Lo miraron
Espléndidas e intrigadas
Leves sonrieron

Un frijolito
Ladeado puesto al revés
Risa de miel

Cantó la niña
Sus ojos se abrieron como
A una mañana

Le devolvió
La imagen sorprendido
Cruz venidera

Sonreía feliz
Complacida de ser una
Vía Láctea

Cuántos faltan
Dos y medio meses lunares
Estela de plata

En diciembre será
La lumbre volcán efímero
El nacer ardiendo

Descubrimiento
Niña abierta sangre mácula
Páramo aullidos

Final y principio
Vagidos leche inicial historia
Que devora parto

Fruto y asombro
Madre que libera otro amor
Desde su herida

Estarán inermes
Como *el grito* ante un mundo
Árido y forastero

la casa del anón
por Leonel P. Bernal

Un hormiguero de raros sentimientos
me va reptando del pecho a la garganta,
devorando las palabras que no digo,
y ésta nostalgia de madera carcomida
y fibras de abúlicos silencios vulnerables,
donde las horas pasan engarzadas
tal una interminable serpiente presurosa
de consternada persistencia.

En el pasado ya pasado,
olvidé la juventud desmemoriado,
guindada entre los gajos de un anón,
donde una vez colgué los sueños
para que florecieran, antes de la partida,
la distancia, el huraño silencio,
y la imperiosa voluntad de los caminos,
donde gasté los pasos presurosos
de mi egoísmo hambriento de distancias.

De la continuidad inexistente de una segunda piel,
donde sembrar los sueños,
o cavar las grutas a los duendes
que siempre van conmigo,
que más me duelen
cuanto más los vivo.
Porque todos los amagos me llevan al pasado,
pretendo figurarme nuevas rutas
para mis pies cansados.
A la vez que cabalgo sobre el tiempo,
jugándome al anhelo la última ilusión,
de que florezca la alegría desbordada
en la distante casa del anón.

ansias
por Leonel P. Bernal

Llegas desnuda y sin secretos
al laberinto extraño de mi vida,
socavas en mi centro y endulzas las heridas.
Es tu cuerpo violín de tersas cuerdas,
hecho para vibrar entre mis dedos complacidos
las inefables notas de tus ansias.

Me pierdo en el entorno de tus senos,
la deliciosa curva de tu vientre,
tu boca traviesa y tentadora,
y la acogedora tibieza de tu sexo.
Tú eres la pasión que se acomoda
en el mejor espacio de mi instinto.

Sin pasado ni futuro, pero sin fronteras,
un diario despertar a la locura
que bebo de tus labios regalados
y nacidos para amar, entre reclamos,
delirios, quejas, y suspiros,

cuando desnuda y sin pudores
te abres y penetro, más allá de la fe,
del tiempo y las palabras.
Más intenso que el odio
y que el amor que ansias,
mecidos en el vaivén de nuestros cuerpos,
hasta el orgasmo real de la alegría.

después de tanto
      Lo imperfecto es nuestro paraíso
          Wallace Stevens, *The Poems of Our Climate*
por Rei Berroa

Y es que queremos saber
qué va a pasar después de este programa en que vivimos,
si el parte informativo nos traerá las mismas pesadumbres,
o si las infelices falacias del político
unirán a la oposición y harán que vuelva a nuestro lado.

Nadie sabe qué va a ser de la correa
que llevábamos atada a la cintura,
quién se quedará por fin con las llaves de la casa,

qué pie calzará nuestro zapato
recién estrenado aquel mismo día
o quién mantendrá el tintero del estudio
siempre lleno de palabras.

Y ella, ¿a dónde irá?
¿Frente a quién pondrá mañana al descubierto
el comestible tiempo de sus pechos bien guardados?
¿De quién el fruto será
que abrigará su vientre en primavera?
¿Y qué va a ser de toda aquesta humanidad
que nos echaba una mano para cazar las mariposas
cuando hacía tanto frío en el ombligo?

la verdad a todas horas
por Rei Berroa

Como es legítimo pensar

que unas primaveras son más ciertas que otras primaveras,
que llena la vida los pasillos de la casa
en los pies diminutos de los niños
y en sus ojos sin cansancio,
que produce más muerte un soldado
que un olivo, tu canción o este poeta,
que una hoja de metal o de papel
puede cortar el tiempo y no ser nada,
que la hierba de este patio en que los sueños se agigantan
sube irremisiblemente en busca de tu boca
para hacer que la lengua diga la verdad a todas horas
y no se quede nadie afuera cuando hablamos,
que son sinónimos leer y labrar
como nacer y no ser o morir y no reír,

dejo en tus sentidos
el vibrante resplandor de estas palabras
en donde quizás encuentres, cuando te falte el aire,
pasto para tus manos
y sano heno para rumiar en las horas que robamos al olvido.

al mestizaje
por Brenda Cárdenas

In mi gente's hips, el clave
and from mi gente's lips, sale
a fluid, funky lingo fusion
that fools among you call intrusion,
but purity is an illusion.
So if you can't dig la mezcla, ¡chale!

Es Indio, Africana, Gitana, Americano,
Europeo con nada feo y todo vale:
El papalote, el aguacate, el tecolote, el cacahuete,
y las rucas en sus trocas parqueando con los chucos.
Es que muchas palabras inventamos.
Son los brazos en abrazos
y el gas en tus chingazos
that always make us strong.
Es el ¿que? en nuestro choque,
el ¡ole! en mi pozole
que siempre give us song.

Hay un oso en sabroso
y tanto ajo en ¡carajo!
que la verdad requiere ver,
y no podemos hacer nada sin un ser.
En la mente de mi gente que es tan inteligente,
hermanos se levantan las manos
y todos los derechos están hechos.
¡Echale! Es como anda la banda. ¡Echale!

Watcha! Mi Totacha te da catos, un mitote de Caló.
Es la lengua de mis cuates, un cuetazo Chicano.
We call Allah with ¡ojala!
and send Dios with adios,
and the al in tamal feeds us all. ¡Orale!

poema para los tin-tun-teros
por Brenda Cárdenas

Este para los timbaleros, los bateristas, los tin-tun-teros,
los que tocan con cucharas en sus estufas
con lápices en sus escritorios
con uñas y nudillos en mesas, muebles, sus propias cabezas
con puños contra paredes

y dedos en las espinas y curvas de sus amantes, danzantes.

Este para los congueros, los tamboristas, los bongoseros,
los que nunca descansan
con sus tacones siempre golpeando la piel del piso,
zapateando en sus sueños llenos de maracas, güiros y claves,
estos bailadores con pasos tan suaves
y cadenas que se muevan como sus high hats y tarolas.

Este para los timbaleros, los bateristas, los tin-tun-teros.
Son chingones con sus tormentas de platillos,
sus juegos de palillos que vuelan como alas. Que malas
sus trampas que no nos permitan trabajar ni dormir,
solamente bailar y cantar, cantar y bailar
y a veces mover la tierra un poquito.

desde el beso del tiempo
por Fanny Carrión de Fierro

Desde el beso del tiempo.

Desde la suave aurora de mi raza,
la música del aire
y el horizonte rosa de mi cumbre.

Desde la incierta forma de mi estrella
sin rumbo ni destino
y la humilde alegría
de mi primera noche prodigiosa.

Desde todos los gritos,
desde siempre
te he estado amando.

Te he estado amando, Amor,
hacia la tarde,
cuando la magia del deseo enciende
la azul fosforescencia de las cosas
y en la callada entraña del crepúsculo
suspiran universos y luciérnagas.

Te he amado
cuando el ala recóndita del viento
revelaba el secreto
del más íntimo encuentro
y cuando, en muchedumbre, las bacantes

perseguían Orfeos y espejismos.

Y te he amado
en los hijos,
los amantes,
los niños y los hombres,
que un día se lanzaron hacia el monte
a buscar la esperanza
y sólo se encontraron con la muerte.

Cuánto te amé
en el llanto de todas las mujeres.

En el odio al tirano
que manipula sueños
como si fueran bonos
y vende su país
por un mezquino plato de lentejas,
y en mi desprecio
de las encantadoras muñecas de salón
y los señores
que piensan que el amor
es un juego
o un rifle
o un siniestro recurso de violencia.

esta voz
por Fanny Carrión de Fierro

Esta voz
que me toca con sus alas.

Esta voz
o luciérnaga o paloma
llega desde tu ausencia.

Llega y llama
limpia y cura
suaviza y purifica.

Tu magnolia de sol
tu lumbre viva
tu promesa de paz ineludible.

Alfa y omega
sello y misterio

trueno y profecía.

Una flor
o susurro o pentagrama
cae en mi desolada
isla de soledad.

Llega y canta
toca y sana
besa y exorciza.

Mi clavel de oración
mi flauta agreste
mi sílaba ritual
mi tiempo eterno.

Un gorrión
o semilla o cataclismo
renaciendo renace.

El rocío en la aurora
y la escarcha en el véspero
se mueren sin morir.

Fin y principio
río y armonía
santuario y orfandad.

Tu voz mi flor
mi abismo tu ascensión.

Esta voz
que me toca con sus alas.

frida pinta su retrato mirándose en un espejo
por Don Cellini

Anochece
sola
estoy yo
alejada
en la casa
en Coyoacán
no hay brisa

no hay luna
esta noche
dónde estás

Diego

dónde estás
esta noche
no hay luna
no hay brisa
en Coyoacán
en la casa
alejada
estoy yo
sola
anochece.

Mirándose en un espejo
Frida pinta su retrato

lo que me dijo borges
por Don Cellini

En el Museo de Cervantes
en la calle Atocha número 85
en Madrid

en el segundo piso
en una vitrina de cristal
en el área de exhibiciones

hay una antigua pluma
usada por el autor famoso
para escribir el *Quijote*.

Borges insistió
que la pluma
conocía bien a Cervantes,

las emociones que corren por las aventuras
el latido creciente
al escribir el nombre de Dulcinea

Borges, si es verdad, dime,
¿qué sabe mi computadora portátil
acerca de mi?

No me contestó,
ni una palabra.
Borges no me dijo nada.

san andrés de la cal
por Don Cellini

¿Cuántos años hace, le pregunté,
que el buen San Andrés guarda su pueblo?
Muchos, usted me dijo. Nuestros antepasados
nos dijeron que ya estaba cuando nacieron ellos.

Hoy usted riega agua enfrente de su casa para fijar el polvo,
muele especias, chocolate, nueces para el mole,
cocina lentamente la barbacoa,
gasta un año de ahorros en las bebidas
e invita a su casa a todos que vengan a visitar
en su día de santo. Andrés, en cambio, debe asegurar
otro año de prosperidad al pueblo.

No puedo decirle pero hubiera sido mejor
ahorrar el dinero y el mole, perdonar el toro viejo
por otro tiempo. San Andrés no puede
restaurar sus campos cansados,
traer trabajos nuevos a su pueblo perdido
ni devolver a sus hijos que trabajan ahora
en los campos de tabaco de Carolina del Sur.

Hasta el campo que produce fragmentos de ollas
antiguas pronto cesará su producción.

la luz azul
por Alfred Corn
San Miguel de Allende
Día de la Asunción

Mediodía. Ligeros velos
Transparentes del ancho cielo….

En la estancia una sombra amorfa,
Blanda, no acababa de anunciar
Ese alto silencio que jamás
Ha de callar.

Tan comprensiva
Como dulce, recíbeme, luz
Azul, que colmas los rincones...

¿Pues, inmóvil? No, mejor fuera
Salir en busca del asunto,
La palabra de mortal piedad
Caída como una flor ardiente
Entre las piedras de la calle.

respuesta a darío
por Alfred Corn

Y, no obstante, la vida es bella
Por poseer
La perla, la rosa, la estrella
Y la mujer.—Ruben Darío

Y, no obstante, la vida quiere ser
Su nombre:
Arbol, cavallo, sueño, amanecer
Y el hombre.

lenguaje sin fronteras
por Efraín Garza

Lenguaje sin fronteras y sustento
sobrevolando sin alianzas
con palabras emitidas al viento.

Lenguaje de espuma y de reto,
vocablos en múltiples colores
expresando un conflicto escueto.

Lenguaje peregrino milenario
del versado piloto aventurero
que sobrevuela un valle legendario.

Lenguaje abrigado en su gabán
de oxidadas oraciones de antaño
y de locuciones secas en el desván.

Lenguaje de un místico poema,
inaudible plegaria sin respuesta,
disparate oral, confuso dilema.

Lenguaje de un galeón pirata,
albatros de islas precolombinas
cruzando las costas de plata.

triste panorama
por Efraín Garza

Pintura al lienzo de un valle esquivo,
rojas rosas marchitándose en la colina,
blancos alcatraces pintados sin resina,
rosa y púrpura inhibiendo lo lascivo.

El camerino de un actor de quinta categoría
y el claustro de una ascética monja penitente
experimentan el transcurrir del tiempo presente,
los segundos, los minutos y las horas del día.

Lluvia ácida de la ignorancia enclaustrada,
hiedra húmeda en la ribera de los ríos,
filosofías congeladas por los gélidos fríos,
trágicas secuelas de la nefasta temporada.

Orgullosa luciendo su oceánica sabiduría
navega la gaviota y sus pensamientos
surcan abúlicos los cielos cenicientos
del levante al ocaso, de la noche al día.

lejos de todos
por Robert L. Girón

Lejos de todos
 *esclavado en mi mente
sin cualquier alma
 veo pasar los hombres
de fuego y hierro

...la guerra conozco como mi dama
¡ jamás pensé !
 ¿porqué no decirlo...?

el sol perdió su fuego
y siento mis muslos
       temblar
          de
             f
                r
                   í
                      o

* combinación de esclavo y clavado

a ritmo de discoteca
por Juan M. Godoy

Porque fuera de este lugar
no hay paraíso posible.
Subterráneo, donde horizontales estiletes
desgarran cuerpos de relámpago, todo luz y movimiento.

Cuando silenciosamente sobrevuelan
la planicie verde-espuma enmoquetada,
y con pie resuelto, buscan
en la trasnochada mirada del siguiente extraño
una canción que bucee por sus venas.

Con las cabezas cortadas,
los ojos en blanco,
y el éxtasis de aquellos que se disponen a recibir el estigma,
seguirán el ritmo con una adquirida convicción de años.

Otros, con pretendida indiferencia,
observarán el espectáculo
de los sumergidos y monótonos
bailes del ritual.

Pero incluso éstos,
sin dramatismo, al unisono,
inclinarán el rostro
cuando tú entres.

Es entonces, en ese mecánico momento
la misma pregunta acumulada en el tiempo,
sácame de aquí o
ámame.

la carrera del guardacostas
por Juan M. Godoy

Atletas sin pista, corredores de fondo,
abrís el aire de la tarde tras deconocido galardón.

Vuestras plantas, silenciadas en un mar de alas nervio-blancas
sobrevuelan los vértices de un sueño, que no es el mío.

Dioses suspendidos del asfalto, vigías de futuras aventuras,
llevais en vuestros pechos de dulce almendra
todo el vértigo de la velocidad incontrolada.

Como estelas pasais sin notar mi presencia,
con el arrogante don de una juventud recién llegada.
Yo, en silencio, os saludo codiciados amores.

Desnuda, vuestra adoctrinada testa,
impedirá que el muslo todo se revele en la dulzura del amor,
como dulces son vuestras cinturas.

Huireis de mi, dejando en el aire la conmoción de
un olor, perlas enfurecidas.
Inmovilizado yo, pregunto ¿Para quién la almendra, el muslo, la perla?

Si hoy promesa ligera, repetidos sereis un día.
Si hoy velocidad, mañana legítima rapiña de ley reproductora.

vi a las estrellas echándome la culpa con la noche
por Rigoberto González

vi a las estrellas echándome la culpa con la noche
vi a la luna abrirse como agujero en el pecho

¿en dónde escondiste a mis hijos, llorona?
¿quiénes son estas viejas abiertas de piernas entre las páginas cerradas
    de la revista?

virgen de la mierda, apiádate de mí
dicen que el moribundo de repente encuentra religión

y la he encontrado como calzón de puta
enfadada con las pequeñas tristezas del mundo

para que declarar mis penas si hasta los dientes me han abandonado
    a la chingada
buscan propósito dentro las bocas de otros muertos

si hablan, ¿recordarán mi nombre? ¿mis pecados?
¡qué babosos! se morderán la lengua y aprenderán a mentir

y dirán que mis hijos me velan con llantos de orgullo en los ojos
y dirán que mi mujer se derrite de risa al recordar mis payasadas

y dirán que me fui al reino de Dios con las manos blancas como la mortaja
sábana de cal que me esconde las cicatrices del seno donde
    me ensarté el puñal

que desgracia morir sin las bellas damas de mi sangre
¿a dónde se irían tan miserables y desnudas?

cuando regresen la puerta se habrá quedado con el hocico abierto
y mi corazón se habrá asfixiado

mira que feto tan gris
le regalé ventana y nomás se burló de mí

el cabrón sabía desde un principio que no tenía garganta
ni tripa, ni culo, ni panza, ni lombriz

ojos de cera
por JoseMarGuerr

Los opiniones de
los perros
no importan tanto
como los mios.

Eran tus plaseres
escucharlos y siempre
los bebias como vasos de
leche fria.

Estos dias cuando
te hablo,
tus ojos se abren
como flores communes.

No brillian de color;
no cambian al entenderme;

no parparean tampoco
y no me responden.

Tus ojos son arcos muertos.
Solo fijan y me parecen
mundos de cera, encerrados en
orbitas de piedra

laberintos
por Marta López-Luaces

Elijo
    lo femenino de mi ciudadanía
    lo masculino de mi nacionalidad
desentonar
      sin acento
      que diga un país
      ni ritmo
hecho a la medida.

Anhelo,
    la negación
    los paisajes que reconozcan
    los nuevos signos
de mí

revisar
    en la magia de los márgenes
el deseo
    arraigado de una tradición.

Busco
    en los mapas del alma
regresar
    a los laberintos

de la palabra.

llegar
por Marta López-Luaces

desde el Bronx
a mi ciudad

desde los ojos
             de esta niña negra
a mi mirada.

desde Africa
a Sudamérica

desde la esclavitud
a la posmodernidad

desde nuestro inglés
a nuestra marginalidad

desde su brasileño
a mi mal gallego

desde este español
a su voz ¿E voce que faz aqui?

desde la inocencia de una palabra
a la memoria de una raza.

manhattan
por Jaime Manrique

Al anochecer, al encenderse
sus luces, la isla se despierta
en su lecho de roca.
De la misma forma que los rasgos
de una persona cruel
se suavizan iluminados
de contraluz, Manhattan
te invita, seductora.
Sus luces danzantes
son serpentinas multicolores
en el entechado de la noche,
sus luces son sus galaxias
y su via láctea.
Pero en aquellas calles
con postes de siglos ya lejanos
aparece la luna
desperezándose sobre la isla
resplandeciente, consciente
de los edificios encendidos
como condos de luciérnagas.

A esa hora surgen de los rascacielos
los ricos, sus ojos brillantes
para navegar las rutas
estrechas de la urbe.

Iluminadas por sus joyas, sus mujeres
envueltas en pieles plateadas,
descienden de las limosinas.

Entrada la noche, los mendigos,
figuras olorosas
que, a la luz del día,
son una ofensa estética
se transforman en
boulevardiers de la selva nocturna.
Amontonados a la puertas de los teatros
observan a los magnates, y sus parejas
abrirse paso entre
el destello de los flashes.
A través de los intersticios
de los espejos ahumados de los grandes
restaurantes y de las galerías
los desamparados, los recién llegados,
los refugiados de guerras y otros cataclismos
obervan a los billonarios
desmenuzar langostas y faisanes
beber vinos y champañas exquisitos.
Los mendigos de Manhattan no
son evidiosos, no
sueñan con probar esos manjares.
Son voyeristas contentos
y comentan: "Qué suerte la
de esos señores y señoras
que comen y beben
esas delicias". Tampoco envidian
a los ricos sus mujeres
encuadradas por orquídeas amazónicas.

Todas estas cosas suceden
cuando anochece, bajo los cielos catóptricos
de Manhattan, donde los millonarios
y hasta los paupérrimos gozan
de la buena vida.

chantal
por Benito Pastoriza Iyodo

la peluca queda en la cuneta
aquel desborde de rizos
rubios ensortijados por la noche
ensangrentados de un rojo vivo
aún humedecidos
por el rubor de la sangre
tacones diestros de caminata aprendida
quedan desprovistos
del vivo sanduguero
la noche la nochísima noche
te espantó te robó la vida
de unas llantas que aplastaron
el rostro que tan finamente
construiste de encantos
y esencias femeninas
ocultando todo el descabellado
horror masculino que borraste
ahora la noche nochísima te traga
con una muerte de pisoteadas
de voces que te gritan
muere marica muere puto
de un crayón esparcido
en la orilla en la calle
la uña esmaltada
en oro y plata
y el bolso que se abre a la noche
noche nochísima noche
en un homicidio
de las cuatro y veinte

borecua blues
por Maritza Rivera Cohen

(La-le-lo-lai; la-le; le-lo-lai;
La-le-lo-lai; la-le; le-lo-lai)

Soy hija de Huracán:
la ráfaga que enreda tu cabello
la ventolera que mece las palmas
la brisa que abanica la arena.

Soy hija de Huracán:
la vaguada que azota las playas
el salitre que besa tus labios
el vapor que embruja la brea.

Soy hija de Huracáan:
con tres culturas
enlazadas en mis trenzas.

Soy la clave que estremece los timbales
las perlas que retumban en maracas;
la salsa bailando en tu alma.

Soy hija de Huracán:
un mango maduro chorreando
jugosamente en tu barbilla
el guarapo que endulza tu lengua;
café hirviendo en tu sangre.

Soy hija de Huracán:

Con ojos Tainos
veo volar tres banderas
en mi castillo.
Con el acento de mis abuelos
hablo idiomas extranjeros
oigo el latido de los tambores
sonando orgullosamente
en mi corazón
en mis anhelos
en mis sueños.

Soy hija de Huracán:
la heredera de su fortuna encantada.
¡Yo soy, I am *Boricua*!

no al silencio
por Irving Rodríguez

Cuándo hay que decirle que no al silencio...
Porque se derrite la frialdad y se acaba el veneno,
y ya no quedan ganas de no tener ganas.
Entonces, me lleno de arrebato y remonto
la cacofonía de mis adentros;
recojo mis quebrantos al hombro
y silbo sereno las notas de un bolero viejo.

Por eso dejo atrás los callejones de este infierno,
para que luego no se olviden que hay misterio...
Hay misterio cuando en un rincón
se guarda el silencio:
acertijo críptico que se va
como se va lo blanco que tiene el invierno.

evolución
por Rose Mary Salum

Tus ojos se van haciendo duros
los pasos se agolpan
sin movimiento

tu boca nace de piedra
oscureciendo los dientes
para conjurar las ofensas

tu pelo ha dejado de volar
                       de rayar el aire
                       con palabras hirientes

y tus piernas se han petrificado
ya no rompen caminos
ni cuartan ilusiones

tus orejas se han cuajado
            de grava
                    cascajo
                          y arena

Ya no eres el mismo
porque ahora yo
soy diferente

buenos aires, 2002
por Silvia R. Tandeciarz

Vení, buscame
en la ciudad de mi memoria
entre esa canción de Leonardo Favio
y la luna, como un tango,
rodando por Callao.

En mi memoria, la ciudad
no está hecha de fachadas
o maquillada de tristezas,
su mascara oscureciendo
balcones, ventanas—
escenarios de cartón
en que ensayás
una y otra vez
esta salida al encuentro
vestida de naranja
el último color
de otro adiós.

En la ciudad de mi memoria
no hay cavidades
que escupen su miseria
prisioneras del olvido
mientras la modernidad
amortaja vidas
en el histérico silencio
de autopistas.

Vení, que en mi ciudad
el horror de hoy no existe
y el atlético es un club
y el garage un estacionamiento
y la escuelita un lugar para aprender
historia
y el futuro un abanico abierto
de sendas y brisas
desembocando al mar.

Quiero permanecer en este andar
Ciudad— memoria

entre calles y veredas, caminar
juntando señas
como pedacitos de papel,
indicios en que descifrar
un nombre, dirección
y el modo de volver a ser
ciudadana del ayer.

ecuador
por Silvia R. Tandeciarz

al paladar de tu ausencia
le faltan moras
guanábanas
chirimoyas
le faltan los plátanos fritos
escalando con el huevo estrellado
el volcán de arroz blanco
mientras en la tele
suena un mundo de juguete
umbral al sueño,
y anochece.

al paladar de tu ausencia
le urge
el cóctel de mariscos
del Quito-Tenis
la arcilla de las canchas
el rebote del juego
la agilidad del judo
que invierte los papeles
el profesor vencido
por una niña de ocho años.

al paladar de tu ausencia
le falta el humo del cigarro
de aquella anciana diminuta
venciendo el tramo
de mi casa a la esquina,
de la esquina a mi casa,
el compás del tiempo
en el recuerdo

es que

el paladar de tu ausencia
me sabe a eucalipto
recién cortado,
a Otavalo,
Indio Colorado.
Me sabe al maní confitado
frente al cine
donde *Jaws* se estrena
y al mazapán de mi niñez
con que me hago

una cajita de sabores
arrimándome
volviéndome
quien fui
quien soñé.

galápagos
por Silvia R. Tandeciarz

Conjurando el fantasma que te nombre
Galápagos surge
en el sunami del ayer
como si la isla
volviera a nacer
caparazón duro
rompiendo agua a cuatro patas
invitándome, niña
otra vez
a deslizarme
por su espalda
sambullirme
en el recuerdo
de tu mano
esa deliciosa lentitud
que es el pasado
con su hipnótica mirada
de bestia milenaria
hecha de sal-vida
Galápagos.

Galápagos
y te paras,
pipa en mano
el humo dibujando nubes
la camisa azul
planchada
en tus ojos-luz
que hoy me miran
desde la fotografía
retocada
detrás del escritorio
que convence
y no convence
que te acerca-aleja
haciéndote más grande que el sueño
que el sol

en esa tierra de gigantes
de enredaderas
trepándome muertes que me crecen
olor a jasmín
porque en el ayer
las fotografías desaparecen
y eres tú,
tú tomándome de la mano
para escalar el volcán
que nos devolverá para siempre
el uno para el otro
el tiempo sin tiempo
más allá de todo
en el adentro
donde junto
tierra-mar
polvito de amor.

velázquez pinta en color por primera vez
por Sheila Tombe

Velázquez, jubón negro, ojos duros, se asoma
en la ventana alta, muy alta, los gallardetes
en la brisa, y mira abajo a la cantería de la corte
(donde un artista, claro, no pinta nada):
no hay verdes ni rojos, sino oscuridades.

Aquí arriba, luz limpia avanza por los techos
y Velázquez nota claridad con bordes grises—
aúnque el gris no mancha ésta claridad azul.

Bajo, en la cantería de la corte, en sus sueños,
empiezan a desanillarse los colores cachazudos.
Se filtran por las calles y avenidas, por las plazas
y los jardines negros. Se rezuman por los muros
sin ruido, víboras insistentes del ojo alto y azul.

A Velázquez le parece raro que la claridad azul
de sus ojos brilla encima de los techos, mientras
duerme la culebra del color puro en su corazón.

borinquen
por Gloria Vando

estoy
sumamente
lejos de ti
lejos del tiqui tiqui
de las maracas que se reían
con tus llamadas
en días de fruto
en horas de canto

lejos del tun tu cu tun
de tu corazón
que acompañaba el tiqui tiqui
de las maracas que se burlaban
de tus llamadas
en días de luto
en horas de espanto

y tú encerrado en el timbre
del coquí
en el llanto de palmas
en el son son son
de tu isla perdida
llamando a tu encanto
llamando a tu vida
con el tiqui tiqui
de las maracas
y el tun tu cu tun
de tu corazón
llamando
llamando
llamando

The Poets

Karren LaLonde Alenier (USA) is author of five collections of poetry, including *Looking for Divine Transportation* (The Bunny and the Crocodile Press), winner of the 2002 Towson University Prize for Literature. Her poetry and fiction have been published in such magazines as: the *Mississippi Review*, *Jewish Currents*, and *Poet Lore*. *Gertrude Stein Invents a Jump Early On*, her opera with composer William Banfield and Encompass New Opera Theatre artistic director Nancy Rhodes will premier in New York City in 2005. She is president of The Word Works, a Washington, D.C. literary organization.

Assef Al-Jundi (Syria/USA) makes his second home is San Antonio, Texas. Two of his collections have appeared in *Poets of the Lake* and *Our Own Clues: Poets of The Lake 2* published by Our Lady of the Lake University in San Antonio. Other work has appeared in *Mizna*, *Sulphur River*, *Cat's Ear*, *The San Antonio Express-News*, and various anthologies.

Shane Allison (USA) has been called a "fag, a nigger and a genius". His poems and stories have been published in *Mississippi Review*, *juked*, *Velvet Mafia*, *Suspect Thoughts*, *Chiron Review*, *Oyster Boy Review*, *Out of Order*, *New Delta Review* and numerous anthologies such as *Best Black Gay Erotica*, *Velvet Heat*, *Saints and Sinners*, *Wild and Willing*, *Any Boy Can*, *Fantasies Made Flesh*, *I Do/ I Don't: Queers on Marriage*, *Gents*, *Badboys and Barbarians:This New Breed* and countless others. He is the author of three chapbooks of poetry and his fourth, *I Want to Fuck a Redneck*, is forthcoming from Scintillating Publications. He is friends with poet, Jarret Keene.

Luis Alberto Ambroggio (Argentina/USA), who has published seven collections of poetry in Spain, Argentina, and the USA, most recently released his book of poetry, *El testigo se desnuda* (Puerta de Alcala, 2002), which has been widely praised in reviews in Europe, USA, and Latin America. Ambroggio was honored as a poet, leader and promoter of American Poetry written in Spanish with the distinction of being appointed a Member of the Academia Norteamericana de la Lengua Española. His poetry has appeared in anthologies in Latin America, Europe, and the USA, among them *DC Poets Against the War* and *Cool Salsa*, a collection described by *Publishers Weekly* as hot as jalapeños and as cool as jazz that serves up "inglés con Chili" and Spanish that "you feel in the blood of your soul". Some of his poems have been included in textbooks of literature such as *Pasajes and Bridges to Literature*. Ambroggio's poetry has been selected for the Archives of Hispanic-American Literature of the Library of Congress.

John Amen (USA) has published poetry and fiction in various magazines and journals, and was recently nominated for a Pushcart Prize. His debut poetry collection, *Christening the Dancer*, was released by Uccelli Press in 2003. A new musical recording, *All I'll Never Need*, was released by Cool Midget Records in September 2004. Amen founded and continues to edit the award-winning literary bimonthly, *The Pedestal Magazine* (*www.thepedestalmagazine.com*). Visit his website: *www.johnamen.com*.

Antler (USA) is author of *Factory* (City Lights, 1980), *Last Words* (Ballantine, 1986), *Ever-Expanding Wilderness, A Second Before It Bursts, Subterranean Rivulet, Your Great Great Grandfather's Puberty Boners, Exclamation Points ad Infinitum!* and *Deathrattles vs. Comecries. Antler: The Selected Poems* was published in 2000. Called "one of Whitman's 'poets and orators to come'" by Allen Ginsberg, Antler has won the Walt Whitman Award from the Whitman Association in Camden, New Jersey, the Witter Bynner Prize from the American Academy & Institute of Arts & Letters, the Council for Wisconsin Writers Major Achievement Award, and was chosen to be poet laureate of Milwaukee during 2002-2003. His poems have also appeared in numerous anthologies including *Poets Against the War; An Eye for an Eye Makes the Whole World Blind: Poets on 9/11; Wild Song: Poems from Wilderness; Earth Prayers; The Soul Unearthed: Celebrating Wildness and Personal Renewal through Nature; Gay & Lesbian Poetry of our Time; Reclaiming the Heartland: Lesbian & Gay Voices from the Midwest; Eros in Boystown; The Badboy Book of Erotic Poetry; A Day for a Lay: A Century of Gay Poetry;* and *Celebrate America in Poetry & Art*. When not wildernessing or traveling to performing poetry, he lives along the Milwaukee River in Milwaukee, Wisconsin.

Rosanna Armendariz (USA) who grew up in Brooklyn, New York, has become a transplanted El Pasoan. She now is a student in the Bilingual MFA Program at the University of Texas at El Paso. She recently attended the Callaloo Summer Writing Workshops, and has a publication upcoming in *Callaloo: A Journal of African Diaspora, Arts and Letters*.

Scott Bailey (USA) serves on The Mississippi Artist Roster in which the Mississippi Arts Commission solicits his services as a writing instructor in alternative settings. His work has appeared in journals throughout the USA. Recently, he can be seen dodging conservative briars in the anthology *Bend, Don't Shatter* (soft skull press, 2004).

Sally Ball (USA) has published in *Barrow Street, Boulevard, Ploughshares, Slate*, and other magazines, as well as in the *Best American Poetry* anthology. She is the senior editor of Four Way Books and lives in Arizona.

Greg Baysans (USA) co-founded *The James White Review* in Minneapolis in 1983 of which he was co-editor until 1991. He has since lived in Portland, Oregon, where he maintains a poetry blog as *Poet X*.

Gabriella M. Belfiglio (USA) has recently completed her M.F.A. in creative writing at American University, in Washington, DC. She is a poet and non-fiction writer. She works as a teacher and an editor. Currently, she is working on her first full-length collection of poetry, tentatively titled *No Marketable Skills*.

Mel Belin (USA) had his first book, *Flesh That Was Chrysalis*, published by The Word Works, Inc., in September 1999. An earlier version was a semi-finalist in the University of Wisconsin's annual book competition. He has been a winner of *Potomac Review's* third annual poetry competition, a runner-up in an *Antietam Review* competition, and published widely in journals and magazines nationwide. He read one of his poems on the Theme and Variations program, a weekly showcase for music and world literature, distributed by National Public Radio.

José Ben-Kotel (Chile/USA) has published books of poetry and fiction. He currently teaches Spanish at César Chávez Public Charter High School in Washington, D.C., and is working on his doctorate at the University of Salamanca in Spain.

Morrigan Benton-Floyd (USA) has published in *ByLine Magazine, Lunarosity, Quercus Review, Manorborn*; received an honorable mention in *Anthology's* 2003 contest and was nominated for a 2003 Pushcart Prize.

Leonel P. Bernal (Cuba/USA) has lived in the USA for the past two decades. His life has centered around the arts, especially poetry and the novel, where he takes refuge and has had some of the best moments of his life.

Rei Berroa (Dominican Republic/USA) is the author of *Book of Fragments* (Calcutta, India, 1992), *Libro de los fragmentos* (Buenos Aires, 1989), *Los otros* (Santo Domingo, 1983), *En el reino de la ausencia* and *Retazos para un traje de tierra* (Madrid, 1979), *Ideología y retórica* (Mexico, 1988), and co-author of *Literature of the Americas* (Dubuque, 1986). In 1988, he edited the special issue on Dominican literature for the University of Pittsburgh's *Revista Iberoamericana* and an issue on Spanish poet León Felipe for Mexico's *Cuadernos Americanos*. Many publications in Europe, the USA, and throughout Latin America have featured his poetry. For the last ten years he has been faculty advisor to the George Mason University student literary journal *Hispanic Culture Review*. He is the literary advisor to Teatro de la Luna of Arlington, Virginia, where he helps organize the annual Poetry Marathon. He is professor of Spanish literature at GMU.

Linda Bieler (USA) has been published in *Peregrine*, *Poet Lore*, *Louisville Review*, and *Hayden's Ferry Review*, among others. *Lessons in the Rain Room*, a chapbook, is out on Finishing Line Press. Her book, *The Outing to the Temple of Body Parts* was a finalist for the 2000 Gival Press Poetry Award.

Larry Blazek (USA) moved South from Indiana because the climate is more suited to cycling and the land is cheap. He has been publishing the magazine-format collage *Opossum Holler Tarot* since 1983. He has been published in *The Zone*, *Poetry Missle*, *Undinial Songs*, *Masque Noir*, and *Lime Green Bulldozers*, among many others.

Jeanell Buida Bolton (USA) teaches composition and literature at Temple College. She holds a doctorate in linguistics and is a member of Phi Beta Kappa. In writing poetry, she strives to express herself as accurately as possible within the challenging confines of set forms, such as the sonnet. She has also written short stories and a lurid vampire novel.

Jody Bolz (USA) is the author of *A Lesson in Narrative Time* (Gihon Books, 2004). Her poems have appeared in such publications as *The American Scholar*, *Gargoyle*, *Indiana Review*, *Ploughshares*, and *River Styx*, and in a number of anthologies. She received a Rona Jaffe writer's award in 1998-99 and in 2002 became an editor of *Poet Lore*, America's oldest poetry journal.

Louis E. Bourgeois (USA) has published over two hundred poems worldwide. His most recent book publication is a full length collection of poems entitled *Olga* forthcoming from Word Press in 2005.

Janet Buck (USA) is a six-time Pushcart Nominee. Her poetry has recently appeared in *2River View*, *Poetry Magazine.com*, *Offcourse*, *Octavo*, *The Pedestal Magazine*, *Southern Ocean Review*, *Facets Magazine*, and hundreds of journals worldwide. Janet's second print collection of poetry, *Tickets to a Closing Play*, was the winner of the 2002 Gival Press Poetry Award and her third collection, *Beckoned By The Reckoning*, was released by PoetWorks Press in the spring of 2004. For links to more of her work, visit *www.janetbuck.com*.

Cathleen Calbert (USA) is the author of two books of poetry: *Lessons in Space* (University of Florida Press, 1997) and *Bad Judgment* (Sarabande Books, 1999). She was awarded *The Nation* Discovery Prize in 1991, the Gordon Barber Memorial Award from the Poetry Society of America in 1994, the MacLeod-Grobe in 1996 and the Bullis-Kizer Award in 1998, both from *Poetry Northwest*, and a Pushcart Prize in 2001. She is a Professor of English at Rhode Island College.

Brenda Cárdenas (USA) holds an M.F.A. in creative writing from the University of Michigan-Ann Arbor and has twice received Illinois Arts Council finalist awards. She is co-editor of *Between the Heart and the Land / Entre el corazón y la tierra: Latina Poets in the Midwest* (MARCH/ Abrazo Press, 2001). Cárdenas' poems have appeared in *U.S. Latino Literature Today, Bum Rush the Page: A Def Poetry Jam, RATTLE: Poetry for the 21st Century, Prairie Schooner, Learning by Heart: Contemporary American Poetry About School*, and the <e-poets.net> *Book of Voices*, among others. Cárdenas teaches creative writing and Latin American, U.S. Latino/a, and American literatures at Wright College in Chicago.

Carol Carpenter (USA) has stories and poems that have appeared in *Yankee, America, The Pedestal Magazine, Barnwood, Indiana Review, Quarterly West, Carolina Quarterly, Byline, Confrontation* and Papier-Mache Press's anthology *Generation to Generation*. She recently recorded a CD, *Poetry Harmonium*, with a musician and two other poets. She has received many awards for her writing, including the Richard Eberhart Prize for Poetry. Formerly a college writing instructor and journalist, she now works for a training company.

Fanny Carrión de Fierro (Ecuador) holds a Ph.D. in literature from Catholic University, Quito, Ecuador, and a Master of Arts, University of California at Berkeley. She has published numerous works of poetry, fiction, and literary criticism, and has received several national and international literary prizes, including the Juana de Ibarbourou Poetry Prize, Lions Club, Montevideo; and the Gabriela Mistral Poetry Prize, Feminine Culture Club, Quito. She has taught at several universities in the United States as a Fulbright scholar and a visiting professor. Currently, she teaches at the Catholic University in Quito.

Grace Cavalieri (USA) is the author of 14 books of poetry; and 20 produced plays. She's produced *The Poet and the Poem* on public radio, entering its 28th year, now broadcast from the Library of Congress, via NPR satellite. She produces *Poetry from the Archives* for the Library's website. Among honors, Grace holds the Allen Ginsberg Award for Poetry, the Pen Fiction Award for story, and the Corporation for Public Broadcasting Silver Medal.

Don Cellini (USA) is a member of the faculty at Adrian (Michigan) College. His interest in all-things Hispanic has led him to Spain on a King Juan Carlos Fellowship, to Cuba as an NEH fellow and to Mexico where he spent a recent sabbatical semester. His Spanish/bilingual poems have previously appeared in *Picante Magazine, Toledo City Paper, Red River Review*, and on the Gival Press web page.

Christopher Conlon (USA) is the author of *Gilbert and Garbo in Love: A Romance in Poems* (The Word Works), which received the 2004 Peace Corps Award for Best Poetry Book, along with *The Weeping Time:*

Elegy in Three Voices (Argonne House Press). His work has appeared in periodicals such as *America Magazine, Poet Lore* and *The Long Story*, as well as in several anthologies, including *September 11, 2001: American Writers Respond* (Etruscan Press). Conlon lives in Silver Spring, Maryland. Visit his website: *www.christopherconlon.com*.

Alfred Corn (USA) is the author of nine books of poems, including *Stake: Selected Poems, 1972-1992*, which appeared in 1999, and a new collection of poems, titled *Contradictions*, which appeared with Copper Canyon Press in 2002. He has also published a novel, *Part of His Story*, and a collection of critical essays titled *The Metamorphoses of Metaphor*. He has received Guggenheim and NEA fellowships, an Award in Literature from the Academy and Institute of Arts and Letters, a fellowship from the Academy of American Poets, and the Levinson Prize from *Poetry* magazine. For many years he taught in the Graduate Writing Program of the School of the Arts at Columbia and has held visiting posts at UCLA, the University of Cincinnati, Yale, and the University of Tulsa. In 2001 Abrams published *Aaron Rose Photographs*, for which he supplied the introduction. In October of 2003 he was a fellow of the Rockefeller Study and Conference Center at Bellagio, and for 2004-2005, he will hold the Amy Clampitt residency in Lenox, Massachusetts.

Nina Corwin (USA) is a poet and psychotherapist, as well as the author of *Conversations With Friendly Demons and Tainted Saints* (Puddin'head Press, 1999) and co-editor of *Inhabiting the Body: A Collection of Poetry and Art By Women* (Moon Journal Press, 2002). Her work has most recently been published or *Spoon River, Nimrod, Poetry East, Spillway* and *Evansville Reviews,* and is forthcoming in the anthology *Visiting Frost*, to be published by University of Iowa Press.

Jim Curran (USA) has published in *Grub Street Wit, Poet's Ink*, and various academic journals. He is also a songwriter with over 200 original songs under his belt. He teaches English, creative writing, and business writing at Towson University. His sources of inspiraton include Clarinda Harriss and Irene VanSant, his wife.

G. L. Curtis (Ireland) has published widely in periodicals in Ireland. He was published by the *North Dakota Quarterly* in their issue of contemporary Irish poetry. A runner-up in the Kilkenny Poetry Prize in 2000, he also has written two plays for the stage and one for radio, as yet unpublished. He is presently working on a novel and a first collection of short stories.

Jill Darling (USA) writes poetry and essays and has had work published in *Bombay Gin, Phoebe, Aufgabe,* and *Poets and Poems online*. She lives and works in Michigan and Connecticut.

Mitchell L. H. Douglas (USA) is a 2005-2006 Booth Tarkington Fellow at Indiana University's M.F.A. Creative Writing Program. Originally from Louisville, Kentucky, Douglas is a founding member of the Affrilachian Poets: a collective of Southern writers formed at the University of Kentucky in 1991. Douglas is a poetry reader for *The Indiana Review* and member of the creative writing faculty for the Kentucky Governor's School for the Arts.

Jim Elledge (USA) has published, most recently, the following books: *The Chapters of Coming Forth by Day*, a prose-poem novel (Stonewall, 2002); *Gay, Lesbian, Bisexual, and Transgendered Myths from the Arapaho to the Zuñi* (Lang, 2002); and *Masquerade: Queer Poetry in American to the End of World War II* (Indiana University Press, 2004). A number of his individual poems have been recently published, or accepted for publication, by *Jubilat, American Letters & Commentary, Hayden's Ferry Review, Margie, Mangrove, Indiana Review*, and others. Chair of the Department of English and Humanities at Pratt Institute, Brooklyn, he also directs Thorngate Road, a press.

J. Glenn Evans (USA), an award-wining poet, author of *Window In the Sky*, *Seattle Poems* and *Buffalo Tracks*, has been widely published in literary journals. Evans, a former stockbroker and investment banker, has also published his first novel, *Broker Jim* and now completing his second novel, *Zeke's Revenge*. A native of Oklahoma, he has lived in Seattle since 1960. He has worked in a lumber mill, operated a mining company and co-produced a movie staring Slim Pickens.

Manuel Figuroa (USA) lives in the San Luis Valley of southern Colorado, a valley surrounded by the Sangre de Cristo mountains to the north and east, and the San Juan mountains to the south and west. He grew up in Denver, and was inspired to write poetry by his English teacher at Manual Training High School. He creates most of his poems from impressions and experiences in the Southwest.

Steven Finch (USA/Switzerland), Swiss by naturalization, lives in the Swiss countryside in a 300-year-old farmhouse. In 2004, *Something To Declare: Selected Poems & Translations, 1980-2000* and *Stray Birds* were published.

Maureen Tolman Flannery (USA) has just released her latest book, *Ancestors in the Landscape: Poems of a Rancher's Daughter*. Previous books include *Secret of the Rising Up: Poems of Mexico* and *Remembered Into Life*, and the anthology *Knowing Stones: Poems of Exotic Places*. Maureen grew up on a Wyoming sheep ranch but she and her actor husband Dan have raised their four children in Chicago. Dan has compiled her poems into a musical stage production called, *A Fine Line,* accompanied by a book of the same title. Her work has appeared in over a hundred literary reviews, and forty anthologies including *Hunger Enough, Intimate Kisses, Essential Love, Woven on the Wind,* and *Proposing on the Brooklyn Bridge.*

Gretchen Fletcher (USA) has been published in journals such as *The Chattahoochee Review, Pacific Coast Journal, Northeast Corridor, The Mid-America Poetry Review, Inkwell, Appalachian Heritage, Pudding Magazine,* and in anthologies including *Full Circle, A Summer's Reading, The Cancer Poetry Project,* and *Proposing on the Brooklyn Bridge.* She has received a number of awards for her poetry in San Francisco, Chicago, Houston, and Newburyport, Massachusetts, and she was named one of the finalists in The Formalist's Howard Nemerov Award Competition. She leads poetry and creative nonfiction workshops for the Council for Florida Libraries and for Florida Center for the Book, an affiliate of the Library of Congress.

H. Susan Freireich (USA) went back to school to get a master's in public health after twenty-five years of teaching, community organizing, and political activism. She went to work in the civilian communities caught in El Salvador's civil war. She is working on a creative nonfiction memoir about the experience. She is the recipient of the 1998 Frances Shaw Fellowship, presented each year by The Ragdale Foundation to a woman who began writing seriously after the age of fifty-five. She has also been granted support and time for her work by Norcroft, Hedgebrook, Blue Mountain Center, and the Djerassi Resident Artists Program.

Mary Gardner (USA), a novelist and writing teacher, spent part of 1991 in Czechoslovakia, teaching English to college students. She met some wonderful people there, and the poem *Ivana, The Queen of Prague* is based on one of them. Her latest novel, *Salvation Run,* will be published later in 2005.

Efraín Garza (Mexico/USA) currently resides in the state of Colorado. He holds a B.A. degree from the University of Texas at Brownsville and post graduate degrees from Texas Tech University. His poetry collection *Acuarela de la vida* was published by Editorial Verbum (Madrid, Spain, 2003). He teaches at the University of Northern Colorado.

Bernadette Geyer (USA) is the author of the poetry chapbook *What Remains* (Argonne House Press). Her poems have appeared or are forthcoming in *Rattle, Midwest Quarterly, South Dakota Review, The Potomac Review* and elsewhere. Geyer was selected as a Jenny McKean Moore Poetry Scholar at George Washington University in 2004. She currently serves as vice president of The Word Works and co-directs the annual Washington Prize poetry book competition.

John Gilgun (USA) is the author of the following books: *From the Inside Out*; *Your Buddy Misses You*; *In the Zone: The Melville Poems of John Gilgun*; *The Dooley Poems*; *Everything That Has Been Shall Be Again: The Reincarnation Fables of John Gilgun*; and *Music I Never Dreamed Of*.

Robert L. Giron (USA), who is trilingual, has published five collections of poetry and his poetry and fiction have appeared in *Beltway: A Poetry Quaterly*, *Poets Against the War* online, *The Texas Anthology*, *The World Haiku Review*, *Puerto del Sol*, *The Great Lawn*, *Art Forum*, *Austin Writer*, *Chrysalis*, *Amphora Review*, *Goodbye Dove*, *Slouching Towards Consensus*, in the upcoming anthology *Only the Sea Keeps: Poetry of the Tsunami*, the CD *31 Arlington Poets* (Paycock Press) among other publications, and is a Pushcart Nominee. His essays have appeared in *Journeys Across the Rainbow: Inspirational Stories for the Human Race* (Rainbow Pride Press), *Speaking Out* (Three Rivers Press), *Living in Faith* (Obadiah Press), as well as in academic publications related to film, poetry, and teaching. He teaches English and creative writing at Montgomery College in Takoma Park, Maryland and is the founder of Gival Press.

Juan M. Godoy (Spain/USA) is associate professor of Spanish at San Diego State University. He has published several articles on literature and his recent book publication is entitled *Cuerpo, deseo e idea en la poesía de Luis Antonio de Villena*. His research centers upon twentieth-century gay Spanish authors such as Vicente Aleixandre, Luis Cernuda, Federico García Lorca, Juan Gil-Albert, and Emilio Prados.

Paula Goldman (USA) has a master's in journalism from Marquette University and an M.F.A. from Vermont College. She is a docent and lecturer at the Milwaukee Art Museum. Her work has appeared in the *North American Review*, *Harvard Review*, *Poet Lore*, *Poet Miscellany*, and in several anthologies. Her manuscript *The Great Canopy* recently won the Gival Press Poetry Award and her collection *Wild Beasts* was a finalist for the National Poetry Series, Gival Press Poetry Award, Brittingham Award and Felix Pollak Prize in Poetry at the University of Wisconsin-Madison, New Rivers Press, and other competitions. She was born and raised in Atlantic City "when the Atlantic Ocean was something then."

Jewelle Gomez (USA) is the author of seven books including the award winning cult novel, *The Gilda Stories*, which was just released in a special 13th anniversary edition. Her most recent collection of poetry is entitled *Oral Tradition*. Visit her at *www.jewellegomez.com*.

Rigoberto González (USA) has written *So Often the Pitcher Goes to Water until It Breaks*, a National Poetry Series selection, two children's books, and *Crossing Vines*, winner of *ForeWord Magazine*'s Fiction Book of the Year Award. The recipient of a Guggenheim Fellowship and of various international artist residencies, he has three titles forthcoming:

Antonio's Card, a children's book, *Butterfly Boy,* a memoir, *Other Fugitives and Other Strangers,* poetry, and a biography of Chicano writer Tomás Rivera. He writes a monthly Latino book column for the *El Paso Times* of Texas and is currently visiting professor at the University of Toledo.

John Grey (Australia/USA), a poet, playwright, and musician, has been a USA resident since the late 1970s. Hia latest book is *What Else Is There* from Main Street Rag. Recently his work has appeared in *Fox Cry Review, The Great American Poetry Show* and *Spitball.*

Benjamin Scott Grossberg (USA) is assistant professor of literature and creative writing at Antioch College in Ohio, where he teaches poetry writing and English Renaissance literature. His poems have appeared in venues such as *The Paris Review, Malahat Review,* and the 2005 edition of the *Pushcart Prize: Best of the Small Presses* anthology.

José Marcial Guerrero (aka JoseMarGuerr) (USA) was carried by the winds of military service (now retired from the Navy) to Mason Tennessee from Laredo, Texas. He was born and raised in the borderlands of South Texas and carries the blood rooted in the Hispanic culture. "De Las Raices Crece El Sentimiento" (from the roots grows sentiment), and there is no better wealth in life than to be bilingual and bicultural.

Piotr Gwiazda (Poland/USA) has lived in the USA since 1991. His poetry in English has appeared in *The Southern Review, Barrow Street, Columbia: A Journal of Literature and Arts, Hotel Amerika, MARGIE,* and other journals. He is an assistant professor of English at the University of Maryland Baltimore County.

Myronn Hardy (USA) is a graduate of the University of Michigan and Columbia University. He is the author of the book of poems entitled *Approaching the Center* (New Issues Press, 2001). He has received fellowships from Fundación Valparaiso in Spain and the Djerassi Foundation. He lives in New York City.

Joy Harjo (Muscogee Nation/USA) has published six books of poetry. Her latest is *How We Became Human, New and Selected Poems* (W.W. Norton). She has received several awards, including the 2002 Eagle Spirit Award from the American Indian Film Festival for Outstanding Achievement, the 2002 Lifetime Achievement Award from the Oklahoma Center for the Arts, an Oklahoma Book Arts Award for *How We Became Human,* 2001 American Indian Festival of Words Author Award from the Tulsa City County Library, and the 2000 Western Literature Association Distinguished Achievement Award. Harjo's first music CD was *Letter From the End of the Twentieth Century,* released by Silverwave Records in 1997.

Her new music CD, *Native Joy For Real* is released by Mekko Productions. She is a professor at UCLA. When not teaching and performing she lives in Honolulu, Hawaii.

Suzan Shown Harjo (Cheyenne & Hodulgee Muscogee Nations/ USA) is a poet, writer, lecturer, curator, and policy advocate, who has helped Native Peoples recover more than one million acres of land and numerous sacred places. She is president and executive director of The Morning Star Institute, a national Indian rights organization founded in 1984 for Native Peoples' traditional and cultural advocacy, arts promotion, and research. Harjo is one of seven prominent Native Americans who filed the Morning Star-sponsored lawsuit, *Harjo et al v. Pro Football, Inc.*, regarding the name of Washington's professional football team, before the U.S. Patent & Trademark Board in 1992. Harjo is a columnist for *Indian Country Today*, the leading Native American newspaper (2000-2004), and recipient of the Native American Journalists Association's 2004 First Place Award for Best Column Writing. Founding Co-Chair of The Howard Simons Fund for American Indian Journalists, she is a contributing editor for *Wicazo Sa Review*, a journal of the American Indian Studies program at Arizona State University. Former news director of the American Indian Press Association, she also was drama and literature director and "Seeing Red" producer for WBAI-FM Radio in New York City. Harjo's poetry, arts criticism and commentary are widely published and anthologized, and her essay, *Redskins, Savages and Other Indian Enemies: An Historical Overview of American Indian Media Coverage of Native Peoples*, is in *Images of Color: Images of Crime* (Roxbury, 1998 and 2001). A Founding Trustee of the National Museum of the American Indian (1990-1996), she serves on its Advisory Committee on Seminars & Symposiums and as project director for the NMAI Native Languages Archives Repository Project. She was NMAI's first Program Planning Committee chair and was principal author of the *NMAI Policies on Exhibits* (1994), *Indian Identity* (1993) and *Repatriation* (1991). Guest curator of the Peabody Essex Museum's 1996-1997 major exhibition, she wrote a curatorial essay for the show's award-winning catalogue, *Gifts of the Spirit: Works by Nineteenth-Century & Contemporary Native American Artists* (traveling exhibit, Eitlejorg Museum, 1998). She curated *Healing Art*, the 1998-2000 exhibition at the American Psychological Association in Washington, D.C., and *Visions from Native America*, the first exhibit of contemporary Native art ever shown in the U.S. Senate and House Rotundas (1992).

Daniel Hefko (USA) is an assistant professor of English at Ball State University. He earned an M.F.A. in poetry from Purdue University, and a B.A. in English and Theatre from Ripon College. His poems have appeared or are forthcoming in *Seneca Review*, *Poet Lore*, *Threepenny Review*, *River Styx*, *Tar River Poetry*, and *New York Quarterly*. He lives in Champaign, Illinois, with his wife and their daughter.

Wendy Hilsen-Bernard (USA) is a soul-centered psychotherapist, yoga and meditation teacher, and life coach. The company she founded, Still River Resources, LLC, produces home study courses and inspirational audio programs that promote health and wellness for body and soul. She maintains a private practice and offers workshops, retreats, and public lectures at corporations, conferences, and retreat centers nationwide. Visit her site at: *www.StillRiverResources.com*.

Laura Hinton (USA) has been published in *How2, NthPosition, Bird Dog Magazine,* and *Feminist Studies*. She is the author of *The Perverse Gaze of Sympathy: Sadomasochistic Sentiments from Clarissa to Rescue 911* (Albany: SUNY Press, 1999), and co-editor of *We Who Love to Be Astonished: Experimental Women's Writing and Performance Poetics* (with Cynthia Hogue – Tuscaloosa: University of Alabama Press, 2001). She has published essays, interviews, and reviews in academic journals on experimental women's writing as well as film, and creative non-fiction work in *September 11: American Writers Respond* (ed. William Heyen as well as the forthcoming *Illness in the Academy* (ed. Kimberley Meyers). She recently edited a large section in *How2* on the writings of poet Leslie Scalapino, and is working on a study of women's intergenre writing. The poem *June 15* is a piece from a longer poem-series, entitled *As Experience*. Laura Hinton teaches at the City College of New York and lives in Manhattan with a poodle, a large cat, and her husband, philosopher Bernard Roy.

Walter Holland (USA) is the author of two books of poetry, *A Journal of the Plague Years: Poems 1979-1992* (Magic City Press, 1992) and *Transatlantic* (Painted Leaf Press, 2001) as well as a novel, *The March* (Masquerade Books, 1997). His dissertation on American gay poetry since World War II received the 1998 Paul Monette Award from The Graduate School, C.U.N.Y. He also holds an M.A. in creative writing in poetry from the City College of New York where he studied with William Matthews and Ann Lauterbach. He has written book reviews and essays and his stories and memoir pieces have appeared in the *Harrington Gay Men's Fiction Quarterly, Rebel Yell, Mama's Boy, When Love Lasts Forever, Walking Higher,* and *I Do, I Don't*. His poetry has appeared in magazines such as *Art and Understanding, Barrow Street, Bay Windows, Body Positive, Christopher Street, Found Object, Men's Style, Phoebe, Provincetown Magazine, Rhino, The Harvard Gay & Lesbian Review, The James White Review, The Literary Review, The Piedmont Literary Review,* and *The William and Mary Review*. His verse has appeared in anthologies such as *Bend, Don't Shatter, Jugular Defenses, Poets for Life: 76 Poets Respond to AIDS,* and *The Columbia Anthology of Gay Literature*. Poems have recently been published in *The Antioch Review* and *Pegasus*. Poems are forthcoming in *Apalachee Review* and *Chiron Review*. He teaches literature in New York City at The New School University and works part-time as a physical therapist.

Peter Huggins (USA) teaches in the English Department at Auburn University. His books of poems are *Necessary Acts* (River City Publishing, 2004), *Blue Angels* (River City Publishing, 2001), and *Hard Facts* (Livingston Press, 1998). A novel for middle readers, *In The Company of Owls*, is forthcoming from NewSouth Books, and a picture book, *Trosclair and the Alligator*, will appear from Star Bright Books/New York in summer 2005.

Lucas Jacob (USA) has published poems in Willow Review, Anthology, and Maelstrom. He won the Gival Press Tri-Language English Competition. He is currently teaching English as a Fulbright grantee in Budapest, Hungary.

John Jenkinson (USA) teaches writing and literature at Butler College in El Dorado, Kansas, where he also directs the Oil Hill Reading Series. His poems appear in a wide variety of journals, including *American Literary Review, Georgia Review*, and *32 Poems*; his first full-length collection, *The Way Light Gets to Be*, is forthcoming from Woodley Press in 2005. He is married to fiction writer Catherine Dryden.

Fran Jordan (USA), born in Richmond, Virginia, moved to the Washington, D.C. area, where she has studied creative writing at small workshops and seminars, and at Montgomery College. While at Montgomery College, she has twice won the Ventura Valdez English Poetry Award, sponsored by Gival Press, and won a Mark Curtis Scholars Award. Her writing consists primarily of free verse and creative nonfiction, and is often autobiographical. She writes with this thought in mind: "Our memories are our stories; our stories are our histories; and our histories are our lives." She strongly believes in the power of claiming one's own voice, and refusing to be silenced whether by other people, governments, or society in general.

Claire Joysmith (USA) works as a professor/researcher on bilingual and bicultural creative expressions in both Mexico and the U.S. She has participated in and also taught creative writing workshops in both countries; her poetry and translations have appeared in *Café Bellas Artes, A Quien Corresponda, Tameme, CLON: Cyberzine,* among others. She has written and translated books, articles and poetry in both English and Spanish, such as *Sofia. Poems* (by Joan Logghe) and the bilingual anthology of women poets *Cantar de espejos/Singing Mirrors* thanks to a grant by the Mexico-U.S. Cultural Fund. She is also editor of *Las formas de nuestras voces: Chicana and Mexicana Writers in Mexico* and co-editor of *One Wound for Another/Una herida por otra* and *Testimonios de* Latino@s *in the U.S. through Cyberspace* (11 de septiembre de 2001-11 de marzo de 2002). She has been training in the healing arts (Mexican traditional and alternative) for the past five years.

Jacqueline Jules (USA) has published in *America, Christian Science Monitor, Santa Barbara Review, Sow's Ear Review, Minimus, Chaminade Literary Review, Sunstone, Potpourri, Chiron Review, Mobius, Potomac Review, Lullwater Review*, and *Skylark*. She was a 1999 winner in the Arlington County Moving Words Competition.

Gunilla Theander Kester (Sweden/USA), a teacher, writer, and guitarist, visited the United States as a Fulbright scholar in 1982 and completed a Ph.D. in English and comparative literature at the University of North Carolina at Chapel Hill; her scholarly book on the maturation story is in its second edition. She has published many poems in Swedish, including in *Bonniers Litterära Magasin*, Sweden's most prestigious literary magazine. Recently her poems have won the Gival Press Tri-Language English Competition, been a finalist in the Glimmer Train Poetry Open and been published in *The Buffalo News, Step, Oberon*, and *Radiance*. A recipient of the year 2000 and 2002 Who's Who Among America's Teachers Award and the 2004 Who's Who Among America's Women, she currently teaches English at Daemen College and classical guitar at The Amherst School of Music. She also serves as Vice President of The Buffalo Guitar Society and Co-Director of the annual Rantucci International Guitar Festival and Competition.

Peter Klappert (USA) is the author of six collections of poems, including *Lugging Vegetables to Nantucket* (Yale Series of Younger Poets, 1971), *The Idiot Princess of the Last Dynasty* (Knopf Poetry Series, 1984), and *Chokecherries: New and Selected Poems, 1966-1999* (Orchises, 2000). He lives in Washington, D.C., and teaches in the M.F.A. Program at George Mason University.

George Klawitter (USA) teaches literature at St. Edward's University in Austin, Texas. He has edited the poetry of Richard Barnfield and published *The Enigmatic Narrator*, a study of same-sex love in John Donne's poetry. His poems have been printed in various journals including *The James White Review, Poetry Northwest, Poet Lore, Evergreen Chronicles, Milkweed*, and *Cumberland Poetry Review*. His first book of poetry, *Country Matters*, appeared in 2001. His book *Let Orpheus Take Your Hand* won the Gival Press Poetry Award in 2002.

Randy Koch (USA) teaches creative writing and directs the Writing Center at Texas A&M International University and writes a monthly column called *On Writing* for *LareDOS: A Journal of the Borderlands*. *Composing Ourselves*, his first collection of poems, was published by Fithian Press in 2002. In addition, *The Deaths of the Conquistadores*, a collection of twenty-five dramatic monologues, was a finalist for the 2001 Gival Press Poetry Award. He also has work published or forthcoming in *Passages North, Revista Interamericana, The Raven Chronicles, The Texas Observer, Concho River Review, English Journal, Mankato Poetry Review, Sparrow*, and many others.

Teresa Joy Kramer (USA) has published in venues such as *Cicada, Open 24 Hours*, the anthology *Migrants and Stowaways*, and *Woman Made Gallery's Her Mark 2004*. New work will appear in *103: The Image Warehouse* and *Re)verb*. Her book reviews have appeared in *Crab Orchard Review*. A former journalist, she worked in Mexico City for three years and then along the USA-Mexican border.

Bruce Lader (USA) has taught disadvantaged children and is the founding director of Bridges Tutoring, Inc., a non-profit organization in Raleigh, NC, educating students from diverse cultures. A former writer-in-residence at the Wurlitzer Colony, and recipient of an honorarium from the College of Creative Studies at the University of California-Santa Barbara, his poems have appeared in *Poetry, The New York Quarterly, Margie, Poet Lore, Confrontation, Hawai'i Review, Poetry Salzburg Review, The Malahat Review*, and many other international journals.

Mary Ann Larkin (USA) is a poet, writer, teacher, and former fundraising and publications consultant to nonprofit organizations. *The Coil of the Skin*, a book of poems, was published by Washington Writers Publishing House, and a chapbook, *White Clapboard*, by Carol Allen of Philadelphia. Her poems have appeared in *Poetry Ireland Review, New Letters, Poetry Greece* and other magazines, as well as in more than twenty local and national anthologies, including *America In Poetry and Loving*, a poetry and art series published by Harry Abrams of New York. She has taught writing and literature in a number of colleges and universities, lately at Howard University in Washington, D.C. Her involvement with poetry includes co-founding the Big Mama Poetry Troupe, a group of women poets, who performed from New York to Chicago in the Seventies.

Daniel W.K. Lee (USA) is a New York City-based writer whose work has been seen in various publications, including the Lambda Literary Award Finalist anthology *Take Out: Queer Writing from Asian Pacific America*. Please feel free to send your admiration / disdain / criticism of his poem to strongplum@yahoo.com.

Gary Lehmann (USA) teaches writing and poetry at the Rochester Institute of Technology. His poetry and short stories are widely published—about 60 pieces a year. He is the director of the Athenaeum Poetry group which recently published its first chapbook, *Poetic Visions*. His forthcoming book of poetry, *Public Lives and Private Secrets* will be published by Foothills Press. When not writing or teaching, he interprets 19th century shoemaking at the Genesee Country Museum.

Raina J. León (USA), a graduate of Teachers College Columbia University (M.A. in teaching of English, 2004) and Penn State University (B.A. in journalism, 2003), is currently a doctoral student in education at the University of North Carolina-Chapel Hill. A Cave Canem fellow and Carolina African American Writers Collective member, her work has been featured at Cornelia Street Café, Nuyorican Poets Café, Bowery Poetry Club, and the Acentos series at the Blue Ox Bar, all in New York City, as well as in *AntiMuse* and the Cave Canem Anthology (VIII). She is currently at work on *Canticle of Idols*, a collection of poems.

Lyn Lifshin (USA) won the Paterson Poetry Award for *Before It's Light* which was published in 1999-2000 (Black Sparrow Press); *Cold Comfort* was published in 1997. *Another Woman Who Look Like Me* was published by Black Sparrow-David Godine in 2004. Also recently published is *A New Film About a Woman in Love with the Dead*, March Street Press. She has published more than 100 books of poetry, including *Marilyn Monroe, Blue Tattoo*, won awards for her non fiction and edited four anthologies of women's writing including *Tangled Vines, Ariadne's Thread* and *Lips Unsealed*. Her poems have appeared in most literary and poetry magazines and she is the subject of an award winning documentary film, *Lyn Lifshin: Not Made of Glass*, available from Women Make Movies. Her poem *No More Apologizing* has been called "among the most impressive documents of the women's poetry movement." She is working on a collection of poems about the famous, short lived beautiful race horse, Ruffian. New chapbooks include *When a Cat Dies* and *Another Woman's Story* and forthcoming chapbooks include *Mad Girl Poems, Barbie Poems*. A new collection, *Persephone*, will be published by Red Hen Press. For interviews, photographs, more bio material, reviews, interviews, prose, samples of work and more, visit her web site: *www.lynlifshin.com*.

Marta López-Luaces (Spain/USA) is an associate professor of Spanish and Latin American literatures at Montclair State University. She has published two books of poetry: *Distancias y destierros* (Sgo. de Chile: Red Internacional del Libro, 1998) and *Las lenguas del viajero* (Madrid: Huerga y Fierro, 2005), as well as a *plaquette* entitled *Memorias de un vacío* (New York: Pen Press, 2000*)*. A selection of her work has appeared in Italy under the title of *Accento Magico* (San Marco, 2002). Her poetry has been translated into Portuguese and published in many Brazilian literary journals. A selection of her poems in English was published in *The Literary Review* and other literary magazines in the USA and Canada. As a critic specialized in Latin American contemporary literature, she has authored the book-length essay *Ese extraño territorio: La representación de la infancia en tres escritoras latinoamericanas* (Sgo. de Chile, Cuarto Propio, 2001); it was translated into English and published by Juan de la Cuesta: Monographic Review. She is the editor of *Galerna*, a Spanish-language literary journal published in the New York. She has recently finished a collection of short-stories, *La virgen de la noche*. She collaborates as a translator with the liteary magazines *Terra Incognita* and *Tamame* and as an essayist with the journals *Lateral* (Barcelona), *Espéculo* and *Literaturas.com* (Madrid).

Raymond Luczak (USA) is the author of three books of poetry: *St. Michael's Fall* (Deaf Life Press, 1996), *This Way to the Acorns* (The Tactile Mind Press, 2002), and *Sylvia Plath Made Me Do It* (Immediate Sensations Books, 2005). In addition to writing *Silence Is a Four-Letter Word: On Art & Deafness* (The Tactile Mind Press, 2002), he edited the Lambda Literary Award-nominated anthology *Eyes of Desire: A Deaf Gay & Lesbian Reader* (Alyson Books, 1993). As a filmmaker, he has directed two full-length documentaries *Guy Wonder: Stories & Artwork* and *Nathie: No Hand-Me Downs*, both out on DVD. As a playwright, he has seen over ten of his stageplays produced across the United States, including the award-winning *Snooty: A Comedy* (The Tactile Mind Press, 2004). Visit his website: *www.raymondluczak.com*.

Steven Manchester (USA) is the published author of 12 books to include *The Unexpected Storm, Jacob Evans, A Father's Love* and *Still*. To view his work, visit: *www.StevenManchester.com*. When not spending time with his three beautiful children, this Massachusetts writer lectures adolescents in lockup through the Straight Ahead Program.

Jeff Mann (USA) has published fiction, poetry, and essays in many publications, including *The Spoon River Poetry Review, Wild Sweet Notes: Fifty Years of West Virginia Poetry 1950-1999, Prairie Schooner, Journal of Appalachian Studies, Poet Lore, Callaloo, The Hampden-Sydney Poetry Review, West Branch, Crab Orchard Review*, and *Appalachian Heritage*. He has published three award-winning poetry chapbooks—*Bliss* (Brickhouse Books, 1998), *Mountain Fireflies* (Poetic Matrix Press, 2000), and *Flint Shards from Sussex* (Gival Press, 2000)—as well as a full-length collection of poetry, *Bones Washed with Wine* (Gival Press, 2003). A collection of essays, *Edge*, from Haworth Press, and a novella, *Devoured*, in the anthology *Masters of Midnight*, from Kensington Books, both appeared in 2003. Another poetry collection, *On the Tongue*, will be published by Gival Press in 2006. At present he lives in Charleston, West Virginia, and Blacksburg, Virginia, where he teaches creative writing at Virginia Tech.

Jaime Manrique (Colombia/USA) is the author of the novels *Colombian Gold, Latin Moon in Manhattan*, and *Twilight at the Equator*; the volumes of poems *My Night with Federico García Lorca; Tarzan, My Body, Christopher Columbus*; Sor Juana's *Love Poems*, co-translated with Joan Larkin; and the memoir *Eminent Maricones: Arenas, Lorca, Puig, and Me*. Among his honors are Colombia's National Poetry Award, a grant from the Foundation for Contemporary Performance Arts, and a John Simon Guggenheim Fellowship. He is an associate professor in the M.F.A. Program at Columbia University. His new novel, *Manuela Sáenz: Mistress and Slave*, will be published by Rayo/Harper Collins in 2005.

C.M. Mayo (USA) is the author of *Miraculous Air: Journey of a Thousand Miles through Baja California, the Other Mexico* (University of Utah Press, 2002), and *Sky Over El Nido* (University of Georgia Press, 1995) which won the Flannery O'Connor Award for Short Fiction. Mayo's poetry has also been widely published in literary journals, among them, *Beltway, Exquisite Corpse, Lyric, Natural Bridge, Rio Grande Review, St Anne's Review,* and *Witness.* Her poems have also been included in anthologies, most recently the anthology edited by Ryan Van Cleave and Virgil Suárez, *Red, White, and Blues* (University of Iowa Press, 2004). Mayo is also an avid translator of contemporary Mexican poetry and founding editor of *Tameme,* a bilingual (Spanish/ English) literary journal. Mayo divides her time between Mexico City and Washington, D.C. She teaches at the Writer's Center in Bethesda, Maryland. Visit her website: *www.cmmayo.com.*

Judith McCombs (USA) has recent work in *Calyx, A Fierce Brightness, Poet Lore, Potomac Review* (Poetry Prize 2001), *Prairie Schooner, Red Cedar Review, Sisters of the Earth,* and *Sow's Ear;* earlier work appeared in *Nimrod* (Neruda Award), *Poetry, Poetry Northwest,* and *River Styx.* Her recent books are *The Habit of Fire: Poems Selected & New* (Word Works) and *Against Nature: Wilderness Poems* (Dustbook). She teaches at the Writer's Center in Bethesda, Maryland and arranges a poetry series at Kensington Row Bookshop.

Michael Meyerhofer (USA) is currently earning his MFA at Southern Illinois University, and his work has appeared (or is forthcoming) in *Margie, Southern Poetry Review, Chiron Review, Ink Pot, Tar Wolf Review, Re)verb, Nerve Cowboy, Main Street Rag, Diagram, Modern Haiku, Free Lunch,* and others.

Colette Michael (USA) is the mother of six children but also recipient of a Ph.D. in philosophy. She learned, very early in life, about the sense of anagogical interpretations in poetry, along with expanded meaning via meiosis for humorous or satiric effects. To the above, one could include other figures of rhetoric so that poetry becomes a game leading to relief from anxiety and stress, sometimes caused by work or by life in general. Who could deny that it is fun to plunge into a flattering metaphysical conceit when it is understood as mostly available within the creative experience of poetry?

E. Ethelbert Miller (USA) is chair of the board of the Institute of Policy Studies and director of the African American Resource Center at Howard University and is the former chair of the Humanities Council of Washington, D.C. He is a core faculty member of the Bennington Writing Seminars at Bennington College in Vermont. He is the author and editor of several books of poetry including *Where Are the Love Poems for Dictators? How We Sleep on the Nights We Don't Make Love* (Curbstone Press, 2004) and *In Search of Color Everywhere.* His memoir *Fathering Words: The Making of an African American Writer,* published in 2000, was selected by the D.C. WE READ program in 2003 as the book all Washington residents were encouraged to read. He participated in the National Book Festival in 2001 and 2003. His poetry has been heard on the HBO Def Jam

Poetry program and he contributes to National Public Radio on a regular basis. He is an editor of *Poet Lore* and a board member of the Writer's Center in Bethesda, Maryland.

Larry Moffi (USA) is the author of three collections of poems (*Homing In*, *A Simple Progression*, and *A Citizen's Handbook*) and two non-fiction books on baseball. He lives with his wife Jacki in Silver Spring, Maryland.

Ron Mohring (USA) has published in *Alaska Quarterly Review*, *Artful Dodge*, *Maize*, *Pool*, and *Southeast Review*. He won the Gival Press Oscar Wilde Award for his poem *Birds of Paradise*. His poetry chapbooks are *Amateur Grief* (1998 Frank O'Hara Award), *The David Museum* (2002, New Michigan Press), and *Beneficence* (2003, Pecan Grove Press); his full-length collection, *Survivable World*, won the 2003 Washington Prize from The Word Works Press and is a finalist for a 2005 Publishing Triangle Award. Mohring lives in central Pennsylvania, where he is fiction editor of *West Branch* and serves as poetry editor for *RFD*, a quarterly journal.

Albert J. Montesi (USA) is professor emeritus from St Louis University. He is the author of several books of poems, plays, novels, children books, and critical studies. His books of poems include *Windows and Mirrors*, *The Quilt Poems*, *Robots and Gardens*, and two books with English poet Richard Hill.

Kay Murphy (USA) is the author of two collections of poetry, *The Autopsy* and *Belief Blues* and co-editor of *Women Poets Workshop into Print (2003)*. Her poetry, fiction, and reviews have appeared in journals such as *The American Book Review*, *Chelsea*, *Fiction International*, *North American Review*, and *Poetry*. She is an associate professor at the University of New Orleans and poetry editor of *Bayou*.

Victoria Bosch Murray (USA), 2004 Cambridge Poetry Award recipient, teaches writing at Stonehill College in North Easton, Massachusetts. Her poetry can be seen most recently in the *Green Hills Literary Lantern*, *Dos Passos Review*, *HazMat Review*, and *Small Spiral Notebook*. Co-host of *Poetribe* in East Bridgewater, she lives on Boston's south shore, near the ocean.

Yvette Neisser (USA) has published in various magazines, including *Virginia Quarterly Review*, *Tar River Poetry*, and the *North Carolina Literary Review*, as well as in the anthology *September Eleven: Maryland Voices*. Additionally, her critical work on (and translations of) Palestinian and Israeli poetry has been published in the *Palestine-Israel Journal*. She is a freelance writer, editor, and translator, and also co-directs the Café Muse literary series near Washington, D.C. Neisser is currently working on translations of the poetry of Pablo Neruda and Luis Alberto Ambroggio, and is seeking a publisher for her first book of poems, entitled *Fields of Vision*.

Mutombo Nkulu-N'Sengha (Democratic Republic of the Congo/ USA) studied philosophy in Lubumbashi and at the Institut Saint-Pierre Canisius (Kimwenza, Kinshasa). Member of the Union des Ecrivains Congolais Mutombo worked for the promotion of Congolese literature with Buabua wa Kayembe, then president of the Union des Ecrivains Zairois. His poetry appears in various Congolese anthologies of literature. From 1989-1992, Mutombo studied philosophy and theology at the Gregorian University in Rome, and literature of Pharaonic Egypt at the Oriental Institut of Biblicum (Rome). From 1993 to 2000, Mutombo studied African American literature at Temple University in Philadelphia and obtained a doctorate in the philosophy of religion with a thesis on *The Foundations of an African Philosophy and Theology of Human Rights in Post-Colonial Central Africa*. He has taught African philosophy at Haverford College (Philadelphia), Western intellectual heritage including Shakespeare and ancient Greek literature and philosophy (at Temple University). Since September 2003, Mutombo is an assistant professor at California State University Northridge (Los Angeles) where he teaches in the Department of Religious Studies, and the Department of Panafrican Studies. Some of his poems have been published in *The Daily Sundial* (California State University at Northridge). He has written an anthology of Congolese literature of French expression from 1885 to 1995 (not yet published). Having lived in Africa, Europe, and the USA, his poetry is largely shaped by the global village perspective.

Daniel Pantano (Switzerland/USA) is multinational and multicultural. Of Italian and German parentage, he was born in Langenthal, Switzerland. Pantano is a widely published poet; his individual poems have been featured in journals and anthologies in Europe, Asia, and the USA. He edits several European and American literary journals, speaks six languages, holds a degree in philosophy, and currently lives in Brandon, Florida, with his wife and two children.

Benito Pastoriza Iyodo (Puerto Rico/USA) is an award-winning author. His works have appeared in literary magazines and he has two books of poetry and one book of short stories published: *Cartas a la sombra de tu piel, Elegías de septiembre* and *Cuestión de hombres*, respectively. His works have won prizes including the Premio Ateneo Puertorriqueño, the Chicano Latino Literary Prize and Voces Selectas. He is senior editor for and article contributor to *Visible* and *Literal,* bilingual magazines covering Hispanic culture, literature, visual and performing arts.

Richard Peabody (USA) wears many literary hats. He is editor of *Gargoyle Magazine* (founded in 1976), and has published a novella, two books of short stories, six books of poems, plus an ebook, and co-edited six anthologies with Lucinda Ebersole, including *Mondo Barbie, Mondo Elvis, Mondo Marilyn, Mondo James Dean, Coming to Terms: A Literary Response to Abortion*, and *Conversations with Gore Vidal* (forthcoming 2005). He also edited *A Different Beat: Writings by Women of the*

Beat Generation for Serpent's Tail in 1997. Peabody teaches for the Johns Hopkins Advanced Studies Program. He lives in Arlington, Virginia with his wife and two daughters. For more information about him visit: *atticusbooks.com*.

James Penha (USA) teaches at the Jakarta International School in Indonesia. Among the most recent of his many published works are an article in NCTE's *Classroom Notes Plus*, a story in *Columbia*, and poems in *Heliotrope, Thema*, and at *PoetryMagazine.com*. A volume of his *Greatest Hits* is available from Pudding House as part of its series celebrating the work of small-press poets.

Kenneth Pobo (USA) had his collection of poems, *Introductions*, (Pearl's Book'Em Press) published in 2003. He gardens, collects bubblegum and psychedelia records of the late 1960s, and enjoys writers like Margaret Laurence, Barbara Pym, and Tomas Transtromer.

Adrian S. Potter (USA) currently resides in Minneapolis, where he works as a consultant and plays writing poetry and short stories. Adrian won first prize in the 2003 Langston Hughes Poetry Contest with this poem "Side Effects." He was a finalist in the 2004 Foley Poetry Contest and the 2004 Desdmona Fishnet Flash Fiction Contest and won second place in the 2004 Ozarks Writer's League Short Story Contest. His work has appeared in *Talking Stick, Word is Bond, Poesia International Poetry Review, Deconstruction Quarterly*, and *America*, among others.

Emmanuelle Pourroy-Braud (France/USA) is presently a Ph.D. student in comparative literature at Washington University. Before recently moving to St. Louis, she worked as an English lecturer at Clemson University, SC. She holds an M.F.A. in creative writing from Louisiana State University, where she studied under Andrei Codrescu. Her poetry and translations have appeared in various literary magazines, including *TROPOS, The Exquisite Corpse, The Southwestern Review, Talus and Scree*, and, in France, *Le Bord de L'Eau* and *Art et Poesie*.

Maria Proitsaki (Greece/Sweden), born in Greece, received her B.A. from Aristotle University of Thessaloniki. She is currently a Ph.D. candidate at Göteborg University, Sweden, and is writing a thesis that examines the works of Nikki Giovanni and Rita Dove.

Tony Reevy (USA) has had publications in *Asheville Poetry Review, Bath Avenue Newsletter, Charlotte Poetry Review, Now & Then, Pembroke Magazine, The Poet's Page, Writer's Cramp* and others, as well as non-fiction and short fiction. His books are *Ghost Train!: American Railroad Ghost Legends, A Directory of North Carolina's Railroad Structures* (with Art Peterson and Sonny Dowdy), *Green Cove Stop*, and *Magdalena*. He resides in Durham, North Carolina with wife, Caroline Weaver, and children, Lindley and Ian.

Maritza Rivera Cohen (Puerto Rico/USA) has been writing poetry for nearly 40 years and has read her work in several poetry venues and events in Maryland, Washington, D. C., New York, Cape Cod and Milton, Delaware. She has been published in literary magazines and anthologies but considers the weekly Mariposa Poetry Series that ran in College Park, Maryland from October 1999 to October 2002 her best contribution to the poetry community.

Kim Roberts (USA) is the editor of *Beltway: An On-Line Poetry Quarterly* and author of a book of poems, *The Wishbone Galaxy*. She has published widely in literary journals and anthologies throughout the USA, as well as in Canada, Ireland, France, and Brazil. Poems by Roberts have been set to music by an alternative rock band, Arc of Ones, and by classical composer Daron Hagen, and several have been choreographed by Jane Franklin Dance Company. Roberts is the recipient of grants from the National Endowment for the Humanities, the Washington, D.C. Commission on the Arts, and the Humanities Council of Washington. She has been awarded writers' residencies from 10 artist colonies. Visit her website: *www.washingtonart.com/beltway/roberts.html.*

Peter Roberts (USA) currently works as a writer, computer consultant, and full-time father in central Ohio. Over the past thirty years or so, he has had poems and stories published in various literary magazines, including *Octavo, Blue Fifth Review, Ardent, The Paumanok Review, Poem, Tryst, Number One, Ship of Fools, Lullaby Hearse, The Wisconsin Review, Lullwater Review, Bitter Oleander, Nebo, Star*Line, The William and Mary Review, Small Pond, Abbey, New York Quarterly,* and *Confrontation*. Visit his website: *www.geocites.com/peterroberts.geo/personal.html.*

J. E. Robinson (USA) of Alton, Illinois, is a widely published writer of essays, poetry, and short fiction. His poems are featured in the anthologies *Poets On Poetry* and *Tree Magic*, among others. His novel *Skip Macalester* is forthcoming in 2005.

Irving Rodríguez (Puerto Rico/USA) is of Colombian and Dominican ancestry. He writes in Spanish and English and is a professional translator. A voracious reader since five, he enjoys Conan Doyle and Jules Verne to Pablo Neruda and Rosario Ferré. He recently won the Ventura Valdez Spanish Poetry Award given by Montgomery College, sponsored by Gival Press.

Joseph Ross (USA) has published in several magazines and books, including *Sojourners, DC Poets Against the War*, and *Drumvoices Revue*. Currently, he directs the Writing Center at Carroll High School in Washington, D.C.

Marianne Ehrlich Ross (Austria/USA) writes about her life in her poem *Numbers*. She started her artistic life as a dancer, but her interest is in the continuity of creative experience–from writing to music, science to art, theatre to puppetry, fact to imagination. She is the co-director of *Concerts in the Country*, a multi-media presenting company in Montgomery County, Maryland.

Mark Saba (USA) has published poetry, fiction, and essays widely in magazines such as *Phantasmagoria, Confrontation, Under The Sun, Mars Hill Review,* and *Fiction*. He is the author of an epic poem, *Judith of the Lights* (The Mellen Poetry Press, 1996) and a novel, *The Landscapes of Pater* (The Vineyard Press, 2004). The poem *He Was A Poet and When He Died* was the inspiration for his short conceptual film of the same title.

Jhoanna Calma Salazar (The Philippines/USA) is the editor of the literary zine *Prose Ax*. She lives in Honolulu, doesn't know how to swim, and has surfed once and lost both eye contacts when she wiped out. Her husband, stepson, and baby boy love her anyway.

Rose Mary Salum (Mexico/USA) is the founder of *Literal*, a magazine for Latin American Voices. She was also the co-founder of *Visible Magazine*. She is the author of *Entre los Espacios* and the co-author of *Vitrales*. She wrote the prologue for *Cartas a la Sombra de Tu Piel*, an award poetry book. She was recently a nominee for the Hispanic Excellence Award 2003. She also received a special recognition by the USA Congress. She has published her works in many international periodicals.

V. Jane Schneeloch (USA) began writing poetry shortly after she learned to form letters on a page. Recently retired after teaching English for 35 years, she now assists in facilitating a writing group for incarcerated women for Voices from Inside. Her poetry has been published in *Peregrine* and *Hello, Goodbye*. She lives in Springfield, Massachusetts, with her devoted Lhasa Apso, Riley.

Keith Richard Scotcher (England) was born in Croydon on the first anniversary of the Nagasaki bomb and grew up in dismal, dirty London. He listened to Elvis, Little Richard, Chuck Berry, the Everly Brothers, the Beatles, and Dylan who all helped open his mind to became a young revolutionary. After working at a Ford plant for the last 33 years, he is wiser but aging, a sage longing to retire and do something useful.

Gregg Shapiro (USA) is a 1999 inductee into Chicago's Gay and Lesbian Hall of Fame and a recipient of the 2003 Outstanding Support OMA (Outmusic Award). He is a pop culture journalist, poet and fiction writer whose creative work has been published in a multitude of literary journals including *Blithe House Quarterly, Spoon River Poetry Review, Gargoyle, The Illinois Review, Columbia Poetry Review, Folio,* and *The Washington Review*, to name just a few. His creative work also appears in numerous anthologies, such as *Mondo Barbie* (St. Martin's Press), *Bar Stories* (Alyson Books), *Sweet Jesus* (The Anthology Press), *Getting It On: A Condom Reader* (Soho Books), *Reclaiming The Heartland* (University of Minnesota Press), *Unsettling America* (Penguin Books) and others. *A Multicultural Reader* (Perfection Learning) and *Literature And Gender* (Addison Wesley Longman), are a couple of the textbooks containing Shapiro's work. Shapiro and his life partner Rick Karlin live with their dogs Dusty and k.d. in Chicago.

Marian Kaplun Shapiro (USA) practices as a psychologist and poet in Lexington, Massachusetts. She is the author of *Second Childhood* (Norton, 1988) and many professional articles. Her poetry has appeared in many journals, and has won nine prizes.

Lucille Gang Shulklapper (USA) is workshop leader for the Florida Center for the Book in Fort Lauderdale, an affiliate of The Library of Congress. Her poetry and fiction appear in *Illya's Honey, Into the Teeth of the Wind, Slant, Strand Magazine,* and other journals. She's the author of two published chapbooks: *What You Cannot Have* (Flarestack Publishing Co.) and *The Substance of Sunlight* (Ginninderra Press). She lives in Coral Springs, Florida.

Myra Sklarew (USA), former president of the artist community Yaddo and currently professor of literature at American University, is the author of three chapbooks and six collections of poetry, most recently *Lithuania: New & Selected Poems,* and *The Witness Trees,* as well as a collection of short fictions, *Like A Field Riddled By Ants,* and essays, *Over the Rooftops of Time.* She studied biology and worked in neurophysiology. *Holocaust and the Construction of Memory*, a nonfiction work, is forthcoming.

G. Tod Slone (USA) is a poet parrhesiastes and caustic literary cartoonist with a *doctorat d'université* from the Université de Nantes (France). Author of *Total Chaos* (2001, The Peoples' Press, Baltimore, MD), which exposes fraud at a national blue-ribbon high school. He is the editor, founder, publisher of *The American Dissident* (*www.theamericandissident.org*), a semiannual literary journal in the *samizdat* tradition of engaged writing, providing a forum for examining the dark side of the Academic/Literary Industrial Complex, and publishing poems, essays, literary cartoons, and letters in English, Spanish, and French.

J.D. Smith (USA) has published the following books *The Hypothetical Landscape* (Quarterly Review of Literature Poetry Series) and the edited anthology *Northern Music: Poems About and Inspired by Glenn Gould* (John Gordon Burke, Publisher). His work has received three Pushcart nominations, and his second collection, *Settling for Beauty* will be published in 2005 by Cherry Grove Collections. His prose has appeared in

American Book Review, *Chelsea*, *Exquisite Corpse*, *Literal Latte*, *McSweeney's Internet Tendency* and *Pleiades*, and his one-act play *Dig* has been produced by Squaresville Theatre in Chicago.

Reet Sool (Estonia) has published two books of poetry, essays, scholarly articles, and poems both at home and abroad (Finland, France, Canada, and the USA), won a few awards, and spent some time as an American Council of Learned Societies and Fulbright scholar at the University of Michigan in Ann Arbor and the University of California in Berkeley. She lives with her younger child and teaches American literature, James Joyce, and literary theory (among other things) at the Department of English of the University of Tartu.

Laurel Speer (USA) has been publishing poetry in literary magazines for more than forty years. She's also a retired reviewer and *Small Press Review* columnist.

Judith Strasser (USA) is the author of a memoir entitled *Black Eye: Escaping a Marriage, Writing a Life* and a poetry chapbook, *Sand Island Succession: Poems of the Apostles*. Her poems and essays have appeared in *Poetry*, *The Kenyon Review*, *Prairie Schooner*, *Witness*, and many other literary magazines. Strasser teaches poetry and memoir writing workshops for children and adults in Wisconsin and around the country.

Dan Stryk (USA) teaches world literature and creative writing at Virginia Intermont College in Bristol and is the author of five collections of poems and prose parables, including *The Artist and the Crow* (Purdue University Press). Recent poems and prose pieces are in such publications as *Shenandoah, Ontario Review, Harvard Review, New York Quarterly*, and his work is represented in the anthology *Common Wealth: Contemporary Poets of Virginia* (University of Virginia Press, 2003). He is a recipient of an NEA Poetry Fellowship.

John Sweet (USA), 36, married, father of two, has been writing for over 20 years, publishing for over 15. His first full-length collection, *Human Cathedrals*, is available from *www.ravennapress.com*.

Silvia R. Tandeciarz (Argentina/USA) teaches Hispanic Cultural Studies at the College of William and Mary in Virginia. A specialist in post-dictatorship cultural production, she has published a number of essays in scholarly journals, as well as translations of poetry and criticism. A recipient of the Clarence Urmy Prize for Poetry (Stanford University) and the *Voces Selectas* prize for poetry (Luz Bilingual Publishing), her first collection of poems, *Exorcismos* (Madrid: Betania) appeared in 2000.

Hilary Tham (Malaysia/USA), who grew up in Malaysia, moved to the USA upon marriage to an American Peace Corps volunteer. She is the author of nine books of poetry and a book of memoirs, Editor-in-chief for

Word Works, Inc., and poetry editor for the *Potomac Review*, she received a 2001 grant for Literary Excellence from the Virginia Commission for the Arts and has been featured on NPR and Maryland Public Television.

Sheila Tombe (Northern Ireland/USA) has studied in Scotland, Spain, and the USA, receiving her Ph. D. in comparative literature from the University of South Carolina in 1993. She has taught English in Spain and Spanish in Japan, but now is an associate professor of English at USC Beaufort, where she specializes in Shakespeare. She is editor of *Apostrophe: USCB Journal of the Arts*, and actor for Lowcountry Shakespeare and Beaufort Repertory Company (recent roles include Shirley Valentine and Lady Macbeth). She won the Gival Press Tri-Language Spanish Competition. Her poetry (in English) has been published in *Rosebud, Yemassee, Fortnight* (Northern Ireland), *Mindful Living*, and *Essence of Beaufort*.

Gloria Vando (Puerto Rico/USA) won the 2003 Best Poetry Book Award from the Latino Literary Hall of Fame and the Alice Fay Di Castagnola Award from the Poetry Society of America. Her most recent book is *Shadows and Supposes* (Arte Público Press, 2002). Her first book, *Promesas: Geography of the Impossible*, was a Walt Whitman finalist and won the Thorpe Menn Book Award. *Moving Targets*, a poetry sequence, was adapted for the stage and presented in New York City by MultiStages. Vando is editor of *Spud Songs: An Anthology of Potato Poems* (to benefit Hunger Relief) and the *Helicon Nine Reader*. She is publisher/editor of Helicon Nine Editions, a small press she founded in 1977, for which she received the Kansas Governor's Arts Award. In 1992 she and her husband, Bill Hickok, founded The Writers Place, a literary center in the heart of Kansas City.

Shelley Ann Wake (Australia) is a full-time author, poet, and essayist. Her work has been published in various magazines, ezines, and anthologies in Australia, Great Britain, Canada, and the USA. She is currently completing a Master of Arts in professional writing and working on her second collection of short fiction.

Davi Walders (USA) is a poet, writer, and educator whose poetry and prose have been published in more than 150 anthologies. Her latest poetry collection, *Gifts*, was commissioned by the Milton Murray Foundation for Philanthropy and presented by the Carnegie Corporation to its Andrew Carnegie Medal of Philanthropy recipients. Her work has been read by Garrison Keillor on Writer's Almanac. She developed and directs the Vital Signs Poetry Project at NIH and its Children's Inn which was funded by The Witter Bynner Foundation for Poetry. She received Hadassah of Greater Washington's 2002 Myrtle Wreath Award for this work.

Amelia Walker (Australia) is a South Australian nurse and poet with one collection published, *Fat Streets and Lots of Squares* (2003). She has also performed widely throughout Australia as a spoken word artist, including the Overload Poetry Festival and the 2003 Adelaide Big Day Out.

Jeff Walt (USA) was nominated for 2003 and 2004 Pushcart Prizes. His poetry is forthcoming or recently appeared in *Runes, The Comstock Review, Hawai'i Review, Americas Review, Bamboo Ridge, Harpur Palate, Connecticut Review*, and the *Gay & Lesbian Review*. He twice won the Gival Press Oscar Wilde Poetry Award. Visit his website: *www.jeffwalt.com*.

Charlotte Gould Warren (India/USA), born in India, lives in Washington State. Her book, *Gandhi's Lap* won The Washington Prize for poetry from Word Works in Washington, D.C. Her poems have appeared on Seattle buses as well as in journals such as *Orion, Crosscurrents, The Spoon River Review* and *Kansas Quarterly*. Warren's poems were selected for the *Miller Cabin Poetry Anthology* and *15 Seattle Book*. She received her MFA from Vermont College, and has taught at Peninsula College in Washington State. She is married, with two grown sons.

Allison Whittenberg (USA), a native Philadelphian, is an avid dancer and former model and disc jockey. She is the author of a poetry chapbook entitled *The Bard of Philadelphia* (Rosewater Press). Her novel *Sweet Thang* will be published in 2006 by Random House.

Fred A. Wilcox (USA) is an honors graduate of the Iowa Writers Workshop. He is an associate professor in the Writing Department at Ithaca College and is the author of several books, including *Waiting for An Army to Die: The Tragedy of Agent Orange*.

Jill Williams (USA) divides her time between Vancouver, British Columbia and Sedona, Arizona. Author of a Broadway musical (*Rainbow Jones*) and three nonfiction books, she has been published in numerous journals and mainstream magazines. Her poetry books include *The Nature Sonnets* (Gival Press, 2001) and *A Weakness For Men* (Woodley & Watts, 2003). Visit her website: *www.jillwilliams.com*.

A. D. Winans (USA) is a native San Francisco poet, a member of PEN, and a graduate of San Francisco State University. He is the former editor and publisher of *Second Coming*. He has published over forty books and chapbooks of poetry and prose. His work has been published world-wide and has been translated into eight languages.

Ernie Wormwood (USA) is a member of the Squaw Valley Community of Writers. She lives in Leonardtown, Maryland. Her work has appeared in *YAWP, The Antietam Review, Beltway Online Journal*, and *The Squaw Valley Review*.

Gerard Wozek (USA) is the author of *Dervish* which won the Second Annual Gival Press Poetry Award. His prose and poetry have been widely published in journals and anthologies and translated into two stage productions produced through Lionheart Theatre in Chicago. He teaches writing and the humanites at Robert Morris College in Chicago. His most recent collection, *Reunion and other Spoken Word Poems* (Pulpbits, 2004), features a selection of his poetry video narratives.

H. E. Wright (USA) has published recently in *Mississippi Review*, *Slant*, *Karamu*, and *The Cream City Review*. She won the Gival Press Tri-Language English Competition and her poetry chapbook, *Tucked-in Shirt*, won the 2003 Permafrost Chapbook Competition. She lives in her native Utah, where you can take your guns to church but you can't marry the person you've loved for twenty years.

Katharina Yakovina (Ukraine/Russia) currently lives in St. Petersburg. Her short story *The main words* was selected for publication in *The World Healing Book*, which represents two international anthologies of poetry, art, essays, short stories and photos by His Holiness the Dalai Lama, Sufi Master Muhammed Zuhri, Rabbi Michael Lerner, poet laureates Lawrence Ferlinghetti and Rita Dove, among others. She participated in the 2003 World Poetry Day in Unesco, Italy, and her poems were represented in Galeria Art i Joc, Citadella de Menorca in 2004. Visit her website: *www.tcart.com*.

Books Available from Gival Press

A Change of Heart by David Garrett Izzo
 1st edition, ISBN 1-928589-18-9, $20.00

 A historical novel about Aldous Huxley and his circle "astonishingly alive and accurate."
 — Roger Lathbury, George Mason University

An Interdisciplinary Introduction to Women's Studies
 Edited by Brianne Friel & Robert L. Giron
 1st edition, ISBN 1-928589-29-4, $25.00

 A succinct collection of articles written for the college student of women's studies, covering a variety of disciplines from politics to philosophy.

Bones Washed With Wine: Flint Shards from Sussex and Bliss by Jeff Mann
 1st edition, ISBN 1-928589-14-6, $15.00

 A special collection of lyric intensity, including the 1999 Gival Press Poetry Award winning collection. Jeff Mann is "a poet to treasure both for the wealth of his language and the generosity of his spirit."
 — Edward Falco, author of *Acid*

Canciones para sola cuerda / Songs for a Single String by Jesús Gardea;
 English translation by Robert L. Giron
 1st edition, ISBN 1-928589-09-X, $15.00

 A moving collection of love poems, with echoes of *Neruda à la Mexicana* as Gardea writes about the primeval quest for the perfect woman. "The free verse...evokes the quality and forms of cante hondo, emphasizing the emotional interplay of human voice and guitar."
 — Elizabeth Huergo, Montgomery College

Dead Time / Tiempo muerto by Carlos Rubio
 1st edition, ISBN 1-928589-17-0, $21.00

 Winner of the Silver Award for Translation - 2003 *ForeWord Magazine*'s Book of the Year. This bilingual (English/Spanish) novel is "an unusual tale of love, hate, passion and revenge."
 — Karen Sealy, author of *The Eighth House*

Dervish by Gerard Wozek
 1st edition, ISBN 1-928589-11-1, $15.00

 Winner of the 2000 Gival Press Poetry Award. This rich whirl of the dervish traverses a grand expanse from bars to crazy dreams to fruition of desire. "By Jove, these poems shimmer."
 — Gerry Gomez Pearlberg, author of *Mr. Bluebird*

Dreams and Other Ailments / Sueños y otros achaques by Teresa Bevin
 1st edition, ISBN 1-928589-13-8, $21.00

 Winner of the Bronze Award for Translation – 2001 *ForeWord Magazine*'s Book of the Year. A wonderful array of short stories about the fantasy of life and tragedy but filled with humor and hope. "*Dreams and Other Ailments* will lift your spirits."
 — Lynne Greeley, The University of Vermont

The Gay Herman Melville Reader by Ken Schellenberg
 1st edition, ISBN 1-928589-19-7, $16.00

> A superb selection of Melville's work. "Here in one anthology are the selections from which a serious argument can be made by both readers and scholars that a subtext exists that can be seen as homoerotic."
> — David Garrett Izzo, author of *Christopher Isherwood: His Era, His Gang, and the Legacy of the Truly Strong Man*

Let Orpheus Take Your Hand by George Klawitter
 1st edition, ISBN 1-928589-16-2, $15.00

> Winner of the 2001 Gival Press Poetry Award. A thought provoking work that mixes the spiritual with stealthy desire, with Orpheus leading us out of the pit. "These poems present deliciously sly metaphors of the erotic life that keep one reading on, and chuckling with pleasure."
> — Edward Field, author of *Stand Up, Friend, With Me*

Literatures of the African Diaspora by Yemi D. Ogunyemi
 1st edition, ISBN 1-928589-22-7, $20.00

> An important study of the influences in literatures of the world. "It, indeed, proves that African literatures are, without mincing words, a fountainhead of literary divergence."
> —Joshua 'Kunle Awosan, University of Massachusetts Dartmouth.

Metamorphosis of the Serpent God by Robert L. Giron
 1st edition, ISBN 1-928589-07-3, $12.00

> "Robert Giron's biographical poetry embraces the past and the present, ethnic and sexual identity, themes both mythical and personal."
> — *The Midwest Book Review*

Middlebrow Annoyances: American Drama in the 21st Century by Myles Weber
 1st edition, ISBN 1-928589-20-0, $20.00

> "Weber's intelligence and integrity are unsurpassed by anyone writing about the American theatre today..."
> — John W. Crowley, The University of Alabama at Tuscaloosa

The Nature Sonnets by Jill Williams
 1st edition, ISBN 1-928589-10-3, $8.95

> An innovative collection of sonnets that speaks to the cycle of nature and life, crafted with wit and clarity. "Refreshing and pleasing."
> — Miles David Moore, author of *The Bears of Paris*

Poetic Voices Without Borders edited by Robert L. Giron
 1st edition, ISBN 1-928589-30-8, $20.00

> An international anthology of poetry with a fresh twist to the poetic power of the printed word. Nearly 150 poets from six continents deliver superb work, from the sublime to the provocative, from the social to the political, in a variety of styles, in English, French, and Spanish.

Prosody in England and Elsewhere: A Comparative Approach by Leonardo Malcovati
    1st edition, ISBN 1-928589-26-X, $16.00

    "To write about the structure of poetry for a non-specialist audience takes a brave author. To do so in a way that is readable, in fact enjoyable, without sacrificing scholarly standards takes an accomplished author."
    —Frank Anshen, State University of New York

The Smoke Week: Sept. 11-21, 2001 by Ellis Avery
    1st edition, ISBN 1-928589-24-3, $15.00

    Writer's Notes Magazine 2004 Book Award—Notable for Culture.
    Winner of the Ohioana Library Walter Rumsey Marvin Award
    "Here is Witness. Here is Testimony."
    — Maxine Hong Kingston, author of *The Fifth Book of Peace*

Songs for the Spirit by Robert L. Giron
    1st edition, ISBN 1-928589-08-1, $16.95

    This humanist psalter reflects a vision of the new millennium, one that speaks to readers regardless of their spiritual inclination. "This is an extraordinary book."
    — John Shelby Spong, author of *Why Christianity Must Change or Die: A Bishop Speaks to Believers in Exile*

Sweet to Burn by Beverly Burch
    1st edition, ISBN 1-928589-23-5, $15.00

    Winner of the 2003 Gival Press Poetry Award
    "Novelistic in scope, but packing the emotional intensity of lyric poetry..."
    — Eloise Klein Healy, author of *Passing*

Tickets to a Closing Play by Janet I. Buck
    1st edition, ISBN 1-928589-25-1, $15.00

    Winner of the 2002 Gival Press Poetry Award
    "...this rich and vibrant collection of poetry [is] not only serious and insightful, but a sheer delight to read."
    — Jane Butkin Roth, editor, *We Used to Be Wives: Divorce Unveiled Through Poetry*

Wrestling with Wood by Robert L. Giron
    3rd edition, ISBN 1-928589-05-7, $5.95

    A chapbook of impressionist moods and feelings of a long-term relationship which ended in a tragic death. "Nuggets of truth and beauty sprout within our souls."
    — Teresa Bevin, author of *Havana Split*

Books for Children

Barnyard Buddies I by Pamela Brown; illustrations by Annie H. Hutchins
    1st edition, ISBN 1-928589-15-4, $16.00

    Thirteen stories filled with a cast of creative creatures both engaging and educational. "These stories in this series are delightful. They are wise little fables, and I found them fabulous."
    — Robert Morgan, author of *This Rock* and *Gap Creek*

Barnyard Buddies II by Pamela Brown; illustrations by Annie H. Hutchins
1st edition, ISBN 1-928589-21-9, $16.00

"Children's literature which emphasizes good character development is a welcome addition to educators' as well as parents' resources."
— Susan McCravy, elementary school teacher

For Book Orders Only, Call: 877.727.5764
Or Write : Gival Press, LLC / PO Box 3812 / Arlington, VA 22203
Visit: www.givalpress.com

www.ingramcontent.com/pod-product-compliance
Lightning Source LLC
Chambersburg PA
CBHW031629160426
43196CB00006B/333